Hip Handbags

Hip Handbags

Creating & Embellishing 40 Great-Looking Bags

Valerie Van Arsdale Shrader

LARK BOOKS

A Division of Sterling Publishing Company, Inc.
New York

ART DIRECTOR	Susan McBride
PHOTOGRAPHY	Keith Wright
COVER DESIGNER	Barbara Zaretsky
ILLUSTRATOR	Bernadette Wolf
ASSISTANT EDITOR	Rebecca Guthrie
CONTRIBUTING EDITOR	Nathalie Mornu
ASSOCIATE ART DIRECTOR	Shannon Yokeley
EDITORIAL ASSISTANCE	Delores Gosnell
EDITORIAL INTERN	Amanda Wheeler

ISBN 1-57990-601-X

Published by Lark Books, A Division of
Sterling Publishing Co., Inc.
387 Park Avenue South, New York, N.Y. 10016

© 2005, Lark Books

Distributed in Canada by Sterling Publishing,
c/o Canadian Manda Group, 165 Dufferin Street
Toronto, Ontario, Canada M6K 3H6

Distributed in the U.K. by Guild of Master Craftsman Publications Ltd.,
Castle Place, 166 High Street, Lewes, East Sussex, England BN7 1XU
Tel: (+ 44) 1273 477374, Fax: (+ 44) 1273 478606,

Distributed in Australia by Capricorn Link (Australia) Pty Ltd.,
P.O. Box 704, Windsor, NSW 2756 Australia

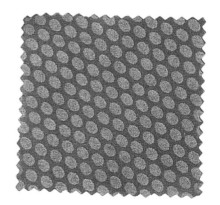

Table of Contents

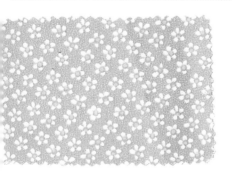

Introduction

I'm sorry, Marilyn, but I most respectfully disagree. A diamond is *not* a girl's best friend. What a girl really wants is a fabulous, never-been-seen-before can't-even-buy-it handbag. Unless she wants two or three said handbags. If you've got to carry all the important stuff of your life—money, ID, keys, debit card, cell phone, energy bar, sweetie's picture, and favorite lipstick (of course)—you may as well do it with flair. Your really important stuff should be happily tucked away in the most delightfully perfect package you can find…or can make, in the case of this book. Whether you call it your handbag, your purse, your pocketbook, or your best friend, it should be a reflection of your personality, however cool or sophisticated or quirky or edgy or dramatic. A handbag is the perfect opportunity to express yourself to the world, since it's the one accessory you can't do without, and the one you have with you every single day. And if you've got to carry it, it may as well be hip! Making and embellishing handbags is really easy and will keep your collection as stylish as the next runway show or as hot as the latest club scene. I'll prove it to you.

A handbag can be as basic or as complicated as you'd like it, with only your imagination setting the limits. The key to a really cool bag is an artful design and a wonderful fabric, and these principles work well for any shape or size of purse. In this book, you'll learn how to pair a fantastic fabric with a delicious design to create your own artistic statement. Add embellishments like beads, embroidery, appliqué, even found objects or hardware to complete your vision. And then, carry it around with you every day on display! The handbag is the very definition of art-to-wear (well, maybe art-to-carry, at least). You certainly need a variety of purses, too; some days you just feel hipper than others, so you need a collection that reflects all your moods.

Did you ever think about buying a rather—oh, how shall I say it?—*plain* purse and using your considerable talents to adorn it? *Hip Handbags* has more than a dozen examples of prettifying a purchased bag that begs for more decoration. (Most of these

poor ol' purses will be on sale when you find them. Trust me.) But you'll also learn how to make handmade bags from scratch, using basic sewing skills and simple patterns—and have fun doing it. I promise. There are seven basic bag patterns that each provide a blank canvas for your personal expression, and their construction is easy enough that you can let a luxurious silk dupioni or a wacky poodle print be the focus of your work. If that's not enough, add a pocket or an unexpected closure such as a pair of chopsticks. Use several fabrics for insets, or a contrasting fabric lining. Zip your bag closed or apply a vintage button and handmade loop. Use couching, ribbon embroidery, or grommets to add intriguing flourishes. A number of creative designers have taken these seven patterns, incorporated some optional details, and whipped up more than two dozen delectable handbags that are yours for the tasting. A gallery of work from established handbag makers provides a jolt of inspiration (sort of like a double espresso in the afternoon).

Let me say this again (and I mean it): The most important consideration when you're creating a handmade bag is to enjoy yourself! Spend some time shopping for the perfect material—it's easy to get carried away just thinking about the possibilities. Touch each piece of fabric and imagine how it will feel snug under your arm, against your shoulder, or clutched in your fingertips. Study its design and visualize it on your bag. Don't despair if you *absolutely must have* a piece of silk that costs more per yard than your monthly cable bill—the great thing about making handbags is that they don't require much yardage. On the other hand, don't feel the least embarrassed if you've found the perfect piece of upholstery jacquard at the bottom of a remnant bin and you paid next to *nothing* for it. This book is totally about you and your style. Celebrate it!

After you've got the material in your hot little hands, kick back and consider the embellishments. You'll learn how to create interesting details with sewing options as well as how to add darling little beautifications to your bag.

Feathers or faux fur? Rhinestones or pearls? Washers or grommets? Can't decide? Well, make two handbags. Or a dozen. Find a pattern you like and improvise with it, creating a slightly different bag each time. Because you know this is true: Marilyn would insist that you have them. All of them! In your own glorious way, express your sense of what is fashionable and hip by making your own handbags.

Design Your Bag

Here's where I always start—choosing an absolutely amazing material that will be the foundation for my handbag. When I find it, I know it with absolute certainty. It almost calls my name. You've got to be excited about how your bag will look and feel to conjure up the creative magic to make it, so plan to spend some time picking out the materials and embellishments that you'll use. After we talk about material, you need to know a little something about constructing a bag, including some basic techniques as well as some amusing options, and of course we'll chat about the ever-so-important adornments that complete your bag. I'll toss in a bit about the tools and materials that make for happy sewing and we're ready to reach handbag nirvana—the projects. Center yourself and let's get going.

Many garment fabrics are completely suitable for handbags. This collection of swatches contains both natural and synthetic fibers. Clockwise from top left: polyester/rayon blend; silk taffeta; silk with novelty fibers; vintage silk; synthetic taffeta; linen; cotton velvet; polyester taffeta; and in the center, silk organza.

Choose Your Fabric

The sky's almost the limit with fabric. In some ways, it's difficult to give advice about fabric because you're an independent gal who knows her own mind. Love natural fibers? Use cotton or silk. Don't mind a little polyester? Then maybe you'll want to use a vintage 1970s necktie fabric. Think about the qualities you adore in fabric and keep those in mind while you're looking. You should be sure it's exactly what you want *and* need.

Here's how to start thinking about fabric: Consider how you'll be using your handbag. Is it an evening bag that may hold only a credit card or a roll of mints? Then a slinky charmeuse will do. Or is it a bag for everyday that needs to be durable enough to withstand the rigors of real life, like riding the subway? Maybe a rugged upholstery fabric is the best choice. Each type of material has special attributes—and maybe a few tiny limitations, too.

Although the intended use of your bag will likely dictate the proper material for its construction, its design will give you an indication of how structured the bag should be. If you choose a tote design, then it doesn't need to be stiff. (It will stand up on its own after you load it with stuff!) But if your design calls for more structure, then you'll want to add interfacing or even rigid lining materials such as crinoline or buckram to make your bag really stand its ground. Remember that the lining of your bag might be on display every now and then, so give ample consideration to it, too.

But hey, don't feel hemmed in by conformity (a little sewing pun there); handbags are being made of wire mesh, papier-mâché, rubber, even recycled plastic bags! Even so, let's take a look at more traditional materials now. The spells you can cast with fabric alone are remarkable. Learning just a little about the properties of various materials will help you choose the right ones for your handbag. Fabrics are composed of fibers, and that seems a logical place to start, doesn't it? So here's some information about fibers and the fabrics that are made from them.

Felt from a crafts store is the perfect choice for this free-spirited purse.

Cotton

What's not to love about cotton? It's washable, breathable, and comes in a mind-boggling array of weights and textures. Its ease in sewing makes it a perfect choice for a first handbag—or a second or third, as a matter of fact. Cotton's strengths are its durability, its density, and its ability to drape well. You're probably aware of its limitations—it tends to shrink and wrinkles fairly easily. Be sure to prewash cotton fabric before you sew. I mean it.

Linen

With its lustrous fibers from the flax plant, linen so impressed the Egyptians that they swaddled their mummies in it. Linen is more expensive than cotton, but offers many of cotton's advantages: it comes in a myriad of weights, from handkerchief to suiting; is strong and durable (even stronger when wet than dry, just in case you and your bag get caught out in the rain); and dyes beautifully. As wonderful as it is, linen wrinkles like crazy and loses its characteristic crispness when laundered (so you really *don't* want to get caught in the rain with your linen purse). But these are less important considerations for a bag than a garment, because after all, you won't be wearing it, will you?

Hemp

Hemp is certainly hip (you know what it's made from) and relatively new on the apparel scene. It's three times stronger than cotton and takes dye very readily. It's not as soft as other natural fibers, though it does soften with each washing and is extremely durable. You'll most often find it in its natural color (which is natural, interestingly enough), which makes it perfect for surface design such as simple dyeing, stenciling, or stamping.

Silk

While linen is lustrous, silk is just plain luxurious. It can be delicate and diaphanous (that would be sheer) or crisp and textured. Because it's just so luscious, silk is an obvious choice for a special handbag, whether tuck-under-your-arm-and-go-to-the-theater formal or sling-over-your-shoulder-and-take-to-the-club kitschy. Yes, silk is expensive, but you don't need much fabric for a handbag. Silk doesn't soil readily and resists wrinkling, but it is damaged by serious light exposure and can be affected by perspiration or body oils. Even though silk seems delicate, it's actually quite durable and strong.

Wool

While you don't often see handbags made of wool, there's no reason not to consider it if your muse commands. (Who knows? She might.) Wool comes in many weights, from soft challis to heavy cashmere coating. It can be fuzzy or smooth, fleecy or ribbed. Wool is soft and durable, but is very absorbent. Like silk, wool has a fair complexion and doesn't like prolonged exposure to sunlight. By the way, it's a myth that moths eat wool—it's the moth *larvae* that feed on wool. A woolen article (like your hip new bag) should be thoroughly cleaned before being stored, as stains and perspiration are attractive to the adult moths that are looking for a cozy little place to lay their eggs.

Felt

Felt, a nonwoven fabric, is wonderful because it doesn't ravel, so you don't have to finish the edges. (Say hurray if you're a lazy sewer!) It has a nice soft feel and a minimal hassle factor—a combination made in heaven. Traditionally made from wool, felt is now made from synthetic fibers too.

Synthetics

Speaking of synthetics, there are zillions of varieties, including fabrics blended from both natural and synthetic fibers. The first synthetic fiber was rayon, which is formulated from cellulose (wood or cotton fiber). Rayon (viscose to you Brits) is somewhat of a changeling; it often imitates cotton, silk, or linen. It's an economical choice, but tends to ravel a lot. A toss in the dryer will eliminate its body and probably shrink it.

Polyester, acrylic, and vinyl are also synthetic fibers. Back in the 1970s, when everything was polyester, you could wear a pantsuit for a year with no wrinkling. But it would have smelled pretty funky, because polyester is not particularly breathable. Nowadays, when you're looking for fabric for a handbag, you're likely to find synthetic fibers in materials such as metallics, faux furs, or faux suedes. Modern synthetics rival rayon in the ability to imitate natural fibers. The wearability and hand (how it feels) of synthetics have improved greatly over the years. They are often an economical choice, too.

So What About…

Satin and velvet and yummy fabrics like that? Well, both satin and velvet refer to the weave and texture of the fabric, not the fiber content. So satin can be made from silk or polyester or clever rayon (there it goes, changing again), but each of these fibers would be woven in a standard technique that produces satin's characteristic sheen and smoothness. Same thing with taffeta, charmeuse, and velvet, just to name a few. Velvet's plush, to-die-for pile can be created from cotton, silk, or synthetic fibers—it's the weave that's the key. And as you can imagine, synthetic velvet will be just the teeniest bit more affordable than velvet woven from silk.

Here are some other fabrics perfect for making handbags, including decorator fabrics that are designed for draperies and upholstery. Clockwise from top left: denim; cotton print; synthetic snakeskin; jacquard; twill; felt; cotton stripe; synthetic suede; and cotton print.

All the materials used in this divine purse were purchased from the home décor section.

And How About...

Home décor fabrics make awfully cool handbags, as you'll see. And you can spend hours in one store comparing colors and textures, feeling each fabric to decide if you're ready to commit or not. (I'm going to call these *decorator fabrics* because it sounds so fancy.) Sometimes even the folks who work in the stores can't tell you the exact fiber content of these materials, especially if you're shopping at an outlet; it's some sort of conspiracy perpetrated by the fabric manufacturers. But all you have to do is touch the material to know whether you like its hand or not.

There are splendid weaves in decorator fabrics that are similar to garment fabrics in that they can be produced from many different fibers. Damask, jacquard, tapestry, twill, brocade, and chenille are all fabrics you might meet in the home décor section. You probably know these: chenille has the characteristic pile you want to sink into, while brocade has embossed designs that seem to float on the surface. Jacquards are handy for purse making, because it's like getting two fabrics in one: the wrong side of the fabric is the reverse of the right side in both pattern and color. Pretty nifty.

This handbag combines decorator and garment fabrics, with a posh tapestry exterior and silk dupioni lining. Better yet, it's reversible.

Fabrics intended for draperies are generally lighter in weight than traditional upholstery fabrics and are sometimes marked in the selvedge as to fiber content (if you've just *got* to know). Companion fabrics are often available in complementary colorways, too, which can be helpful if you'd like to combine fabrics in your handbag design.

Upholstery fabrics are heavier and *way* durable, although some materials may be too dense to manipulate while sewing a small bag. To increase their longevity for their intended purpose, some have backings that make them a bit stiff and a little obstinate when introduced to the presser foot on your sewing machine. That said, be sure to take a look at the dazzling variety of decorator fabrics. There are beautiful materials to be had—great prints, wonderful textures, even some with knock-your-socks-off embroidery and appliqué as well as novelty shirred and crinkled fabrics. And they're usually 54 inches wide, so you can get a lot of purse (or purses) per yard. One more advantage to decorator fabrics is that they tend to be pretreated for stain resistance. Yippee! No worries about a sudden rainstorm or a spilled latte.

Fabric and Pattern

There are a few things to keep in mind about your fabric's motifs. If the pattern repeats are large, you may not be able to capture the essence of the fabric's design on the small canvas of a bag. On the other hand, you may like just the suggestion of the motif on the face of your bag. If you're choosing stripes and you want to match them, you may need extra fabric. Keep the scale of your bag in mind while you're shopping for fabric (or digging through your stash, as the case may be).

The size of this bag was increased from the basic pattern to fully appreciate the motifs on the fabric.

Other Materials

Okay, enough about fabric. How about other interesting things you can use to make bags?

Leather and Suede

It's hard to argue the durability of leather and suede (suede being the finished, skin side of leather). Garment-weight leather and suede can be sewn easily with just a few considerations. First, use small binder clips, rather than pins, to secure the pieces for sewing. Be sure to use a needle designed for leather; these needles have unique beveled points. Use a nonstick presser foot and finger press the seams open (Huh? See page 37), then tap them with a mallet. Glue or stitch seam allowances open. Here's the good news—these materials don't ravel, so you don't have to finish the edges. Do I hear another hurray from the lazy folks?

Alternative Materials

At its heart, a purse is a pretty simple concept: it needs to hold things. So just about any material you can use to make a container will make a purse. Rubber carpet padding, wire mesh, faux grass turf, wicker, polymer clay, fabricated metal, recycled tin cans… go for it, honey. The funky handbags above and below were made from placemats.

Handbags by Joan K. Morris

Lining Your Bag

To line, or not to line? It's really not a question for me; bags last longer and usually look better if they're lined. A lining keeps the inside of your purse tidy, especially if you add a few pockets. Because there are no exposed seams or little pieces of thread to get caught on your rings or intertwined with your keys, linings just make your purse happier. And you're happy when your purse is happy. You can dig away, merrily excavating to find the receipt for your new shoes and not cause undue wear and tear because the lining will protect your purse. You're in charge of the shoes.

Lining options abound. Clockwise from top left: cotton print; synthetic satin; rayon; silk dupioni; cotton print; cotton print; lamé; silk charmeuse; and in the center, synthetic crepe-backed satin.

Choose Your Lining Material

Generally speaking, you'll want a material that's a little lighter in weight than the fabric you're using to make the bag. This decision is a personal choice. Do you want a contrasting lining, or one that minds its own business in the background? The lining material you choose ought to be as durable as the bag itself because you want the two to live happily ever after. Your fabric and your lining should have compatible laundering requirements.

When you shop for lining, be sure to take a swatch of your fabric so you can truly compare the color, weight, and texture. Don't trust your memory to gauge the color of the fabric you've got on the shelf at home. Word to the wise.

Select the Interfacing

Yes, you'll likely want to add interfacing, too. There are a billion weights of interfacing, both fusible and sew-in types, to suit every bag. Usually, the more structured the bag, the heavier you'll want your interfacing to be. Buckram (the stiff stuff that keeps the bill of your trucker hat in shape) is very rigid; crinoline, as in the old petticoats, also provides a lot of body. Hair canvas is the traditional interfacing used in tailoring and has some flexibility. (Yes, it's actually made with hair. From a goat.)

The fine folk at your fabric store will surely be friendly if you're feeling squirrelly about the selection. Tell them what kind of fabric you're using and a little about the design of your bag and they can help you decide which one is best. It's important you tell them what kind of fabric you're using, because fusible interfacings aren't suitable for all fabrics; follow the manufacturer's instructions when using it. Having the proper interfacing is an important part of creating a handbag that looks the way you want it to, so do consider your choice carefully.

Lining fabrics should be considered just as carefully as the fabric for the exterior of your handbag.

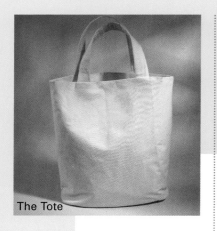

The Tote

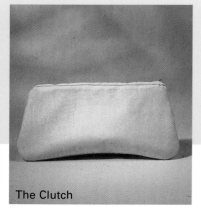

The Clutch

The Tuck

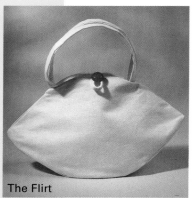

The Flirt

The Traveler

The Messenger

The Vessel

Handbag Basics

L et's get down to the nitty-gritty. What kind of sewing skills do you need to have to make a bag? Just the most basic, really; if you've put in a zipper and lined anything, you understand the fundamentals. Generally, you can make a bag in a day (depending on your caffeine intake), so it's not a long drawn-out project like getting your significant other to put the dishes in the dishwasher within a 24-hour time period. Still working on that myself.

There are a number of techniques that are used repeatedly throughout the book to construct these chichi handbags. And the really great thing is that you can choose the details you want and add them to your own bag. There are seven basic patterns—The Clutch, The Messenger, The Tote, The Tuck, The Vessel, The Flirt, and The Traveler— followed by the fabu projects that are constructed from these designs. In the bag patterns and the project instructions, you'll see constant references to this chapter. I know we've been having a lot of fun so far, but now you need to concentrate for a few minutes.

Standard Techniques

A bag can have only one pattern piece, like The Clutch (guess what it looks like?). Most of the designs have just three: a bag piece (from which you'll cut both the front and the back of the bag), a bottom piece (square or round perhaps), and straps (or handles). *Very* simple. Here are some common construction methods that will transform these pieces into your new handbag. Since I've convinced you that you must line your bag, let's start there.

Add a Lining

Basically, you construct the lining with the same pattern pieces that you use to make the bag. There are two methods of lining used in the bag patterns. The first, Lining A, used in The Tote, The Tuck, The Vessel, and The Flirt, is stitched in place with your sewing machine. Lining B is whipstitched to a zipper by hand.

LINING A

1. First, stitch the front and back bag lining pieces together, right sides facing. Then add the bottom lining piece, again with right sides together, but *leave a 5-inch section open in the bottom* (figure 1). Don't forget the little bit in italics or you'll be sorry. Trim the seams and press them open. Leave the lining wrong side out.

2. With right sides together, slip the lining over the bag and align the top edges. Pin them together, making sure the handles are between the fabric and the lining and not caught in the seam allowance. Match the side seams. Stitch (figure 2), then trim the seam and clip the curves.

3. Turn the bag right side out through the 5-inch opening in the bottom of the lining (figure 3). That's why you shouldn't forget that little bit in italics in step 1! Stitch the opening closed by hand or machine. Push the lining into the bag and press the top edge. Topstitch if you want to.

Figure 2

Figure 1

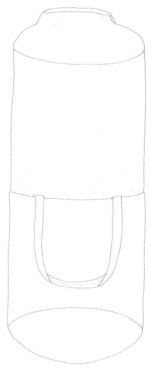

Figure 3

17

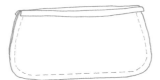

Figure 4

Figure 5

Zip Tip

You probably already know this, but you can easily make a nylon coil zipper shorter to fit in any size opening your little heart desires. All you need to do is stitch across the bottom of the zipper a few times where you want it to end, making your own zipper stop, and then cut off the excess length of the zipper. I'm still working on making a zipper *longer*.

LINING B

In The Clutch and The Traveler, two bags with zipper closures, the lining is stitched to the zipper tape by hand.

1. Take the lining pieces and construct them as you do the bag, with right sides together, but leave the top edge open (where the zipper is on the handbag). Stitch in from the edge for 1 inch (figure 4); clip any curves.

2. Turn the seam allowance under on the open portion of the lining and press. Leave the lining wrong side out (figure 5). Place it inside the bag, matching the seams. Whipstitch the pressed edge of the lining to the zipper tape, hiding the stitches as much as possible.

So while we're talking about zippers, let's learn how to…

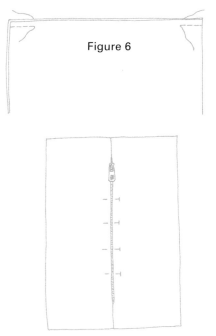

Figure 6

Figure 7

Install a Zipper

This technique works very well for zippers in handbags. It's used in the basic patterns for The Clutch and The Traveler. Here's the best part— it's *muy* easy too. Only two steps.

1. Place the appropriate fabric pieces right sides together and pin them in place along the edge where you'll install the zipper. From each edge, stitch for 1 inch, leaving the middle open (figure 6).

2. Press the seam open, turning under the raw edges in the middle. Place the zipper under the pressed edges and pin in place (figure 7). Use your zipper foot and begin stitching at the top of the zipper and continue down one side until you reach the end of the zipper. Lift the zipper foot, leaving the needle in the down position, and pivot the fabric. Lower the zipper foot and stitch across the bottom of the zipper. Pivot again, stitch back up the other side of the zipper, pivot, and stitch across the top (figure 8). Check to make sure the zipper runs freely.

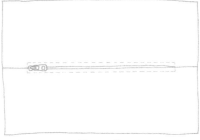

Figure 8

Use a variety of hooks to attach straps to your handbag.

Add a Strap

If it's long, it's a strap; if it's shorter, it's a handle, but the method is the same to make your own from fabric. Here are several variations. Ask your bag which one it wants.

STRAP A

1. To make the straps, first apply fusible interfacing to the wrong sides of each piece. Fold one strap piece in half lengthwise, right sides together. Stitch the length of the strap, pivot at the corner, and stitch across one end (figure 9). Repeat for the second strap. Turn the straps inside out through the open end.

2. Now that you've turned the straps, trim the seam from the short ends so each strap has two open ends with raw edges. Press both pieces flat with seam in the center (figure 10).

3. Pin the straps to the bag as desired, right sides together. You'll be looking at the seam in the strap if you've got it right. Be sure the straps are situated as shown (figure 11).

If you use fairly heavy or stiff fabric, which you certainly might for a handbag, don't, don't, *don't* try to make long straps or handles by turning them inside out. It makes for a very unhappy afternoon of sewing, because they're very difficult to turn. Use the more agreeable technique that follows.

STRAP B

An easy way to make a strap is to simply fold the edges in, fold in half, and stitch. This works well for skinny little straps or little skinny loops, both used in The Flirt.

1. To make the straps, fold the pieces in half lengthwise, wrong sides together, and press. Fold the two raw edges into the pressed crease in the center and press again (figure 12).

2. Fold the strap in half again, lengthwise, and stitch as close to the edge as you can (figure 13). *Très facile.*

Figure 9

Figure 10

Figure 11

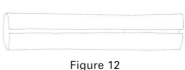

Figure 12

Figure 13

Figure 14

Figure 15

Figure 16

Figure 17

STRAP C

An alternate method is to insert cording into the strap, as in The Traveler. Instead of being sewn into the seam around the top of the handbag, these straps are sewn onto the outside of the bag.

1. To make the straps, take the pieces of fabric you've cut and fold them together lengthwise, right sides together. Before you sew, adjust the width of the seam so the cord has just enough room to slide into the strip after you've stitched the seam. Stitch across one short end, pivot, and stitch down the long side. Turn the strap right side out. Now that you've turned the strap, trim the seam from the short end so you have two open ends, just as in Strap A.

2. Cut the cord into two pieces; each piece of cord should be 3 or 4 inches shorter than the length of the strap.

To get the cord into the strap, use this not-very-technical-yet-highly-efficient method: Tape one end of the cord to the end of the chopstick, and scoot the chopstick through the strap. Once the cord is through, liberate the chopstick (figure 14). There are other ways to feed the cord through; attach it to a safety pin, for example.

3. Center the cord inside each strap; there should be excess fabric on each end. Press this fabric flat and fold the end under about ¼ inch.

4. Decide where you want to place the straps on the body of the bag—remember the ½-inch seam allowance along the top of the bag. Pin in place on your handbag and stitch as shown (figure 15).

See, these things are easy. Now here are some ways you can customize your bag to suit your lifestyle.

Optional Techniques

Maybe you're the organized type who needs everything in its place. If so, you'll probably want to add some pockets to your purse. Perhaps you want to add some grommets or a flap to keep your handbag closed. Here are some ideas for the little options that really make life worth living.

Make a Pocket

There are two types of patch pockets used in this book, lined and (guess what?) unlined. There's also a third, a slash pocket, when you seriously want to stash things away.

LINED POCKET

Easy, easy, easy. Cut the pocket piece twice as long as you want the finished pocket to be, plus the seam allowances. Fold the pocket in half, right sides facing, and stitch around the edges, leaving an opening in the bottom to turn the pocket (figure 16). Pull the pocket through to the right side, press, and slip-stitch the opening. Add to your handbag where you want a pocket.

You can also use two pieces of fabric cut to the same measurements to make a lined pocket; maybe you want the inside of your pocket to be of contrasting material, for example.

Make it just as described in the paragraph on page 20. This construction would be fun when you want to have a contrasting pocket visible on the outside of the handbag and not hidden away in the lining.

UNLINED POCKET

Just as easy, easy, easy. Cut a piece of fabric to the desired size of your pocket, plus seam allowances on the side and an extra inch at the top. Make a narrow hem along the top edge and fold it over to the outside at the 1-inch mark. Stitch along the edges of the fold following the seamline (figure 17). Turn the top to the inside and turn under the sides and bottom. Press. Then stitch it to your purse or your lining.

SLASH POCKET

This is like a welted pocket without the darn welts (but with a zipper). Cut a piece of fabric that is 1 inch wider then you want the pocket and 1 inch longer than twice the pocket's length. Mark with a line the place on the right side of the fabric where you want the opening of the pocket (this is the slash). Center the pocket piece along this line. Stitch a narrow rectangle around the line. Then, carefully cut along the slash line and clip to the corners (figure 18). Turn the pocket piece through the slash to the wrong side of the fabric. Press.

Add a zipper in the slash exactly as described on page 18. (You'll

Add buttons, zippers, or clasps to close your purse.

probably have to shorten a zipper to fit into a handbag-sized pocket.) After you've installed the zipper, fold the pocket, right sides together, and stitch together the raw edges (figure 19). These nifty pockets work equally well on the outside of a purse or in the lining.

Okay, we've added a detail for the orderly folks. How about one for the insecure among us?

Add a Flap

A flap is a quick and easy addition to your bag, whether it's for work (to add a closure such as a magnetic clasp) or for play (it just sits there and looks cool).

Actually, you make a flap in virtually the same way you do the Lined Pocket (either version, come to think of it). The slight difference is that you stitch only the side seams and leave the bottom completely open to turn the flap. You add the flap to the bag before you line it, aligning the raw edges of the flap with the top of the bag (figure 20). So while we're at it…

Keep It Closed

In addition to the faithful zipper (you can't question its loyalty), there are also magnetic clasps, buttons, snaps, frogs (loop fasteners made of fabric or cord), and ties. Options abound for keeping your purse closed. When you're planning a

handbag, think through the construction process to decide when you need to add a clasp or a buttonhole. You don't want to stitch your flap in place before working that buttonhole or adding that clasp. Another word to the wise.

place pocket piece face down onto right side of outside

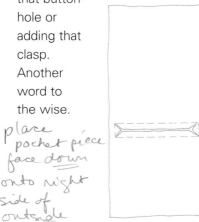

Figure 18

Figure 19

Figure 20

Figure 21

Figure 22

Figure 23

Figure 24

Add Piping or Cording

Piping or cording (one's just skinnier than the other) is a detail that can add a lot of definition to your handbag. You can buy purchased piping or make your own. In either case, it should be pinned and basted along the seamline of your bag with your zipper foot before you line or face the piece that the piping will decorate (figure 21). Stitch the seam with your zipper foot too.

Make your own piping by first cutting bias strips from the stretchy diagonal grain of your fabric (figure 22). Then encase the cording in the bias strips, stitching close to the cording with the zipper foot (figure 23). Then, just add the piping to your bag as instructed above.

Create Fabric Panels

Maybe, just for the heck of it, you want to create panels in your bag. Simply divide your pattern into pieces as you wish (figure 24); a copy machine is helpful in this process so you can duplicate your original pattern for use with each project. *Remember to add a seam allowance to each new piece you make.* Stitch the panels together before you construct the bag.

Add Grommets or Eyelets

A grommet is just a big eyelet, you know. Follow the manufacturer's instructions to install these wondrous gizmos that allow you to attach things to or dangle things from your handbag. You'll need several layers of fabric between the halves of the grommet so it will install and function properly, just as the instruction sheet will tell you. Believe it.

Add Handbag Accessories

There are some accessories that have been developed specifically for purses and you just might want to incorporate some of these items into your happenin' handbag. If you have a well-stocked craft store in your neighborhood, it will probably have a section for handbag crafting where you can examine many of these things. Surf the net for suppliers too.

Handles. Although the basic pattern instructions for *Hip Handbags* tell you how to make your own straps from fabric, you can certainly add purchased handles to perfect the look you're after. You'll be amazed at the variety of handles available, in every size, shape, and color of the rainbow. There are beaded handles and handles you can decorate *with* beads. There's purse chain. There are acrylic and bamboo handles. And on and on. Depending on the design of the handles, they can be added in a variety of ways: inserted through a fabric casing, attached by a thin fabric loop, or secured with purse hooks. Read about these thingama-jigs next.

Hooks. Attach straps or handles or whatever you want with some specialized hooks. Some have bars that screw in, while others swivel; some are quite lovely, actually. Most of these hooks are manufactured in various colors of metal, such as nickel or bronze. Look at a few of them on page 19.

Clasps. Magnetic purse clasps work fantastically and are very easy to install. There are more sophisticated clasps available, too, that close and lock.

Purse feet. Yes, you can get little studs for the bottom of your bag.

Purse frames. There is an astonishing array of frames available with which you can build your bag in any style, from prim and proper Victorian to get-outta-my-face polished metal. None of the patterns in this book are designed to use frames, but they may interest you at some point during your lengthy handbag-making career.

Beautify Your Bag

Now for the pretty stuff. In addition to the embellishment techniques you'll see in the handmade handbag projects, there are also 15 examples of how you can adorn a plain bag and turn it into something quite spectacular. (In fact, there were a couple of bags—actually, it's the same bag, just in two different colors—that are the basis of several different projects, just so you can see how many places you can take this decoration thing.) Like an appetizer, the embellished bags are presented on pages 27–34; they should whet your appetite for the projects that start on page 42. You can, of course, incorporate any of these ideas into your handmade bag. In fact, please *do*.

Many of these kinds of embellishments should be done to your bag pieces before you construct the handbag, particularly if you're doing something like embroidery where you want to conceal the stitching under the lining of your bag.

It makes sense to hide your work for a number of reasons, the most sensible (I guess we should be sensible every now and then) being the lack of threads or knots that snag and pull every time you reach inside your purse. Your work is more stable when it's protected by the lining.

Here are some materials and techniques that you can use to create visual interest in your bag.

Materials

Beads. If you want some extra glitz, bead accents are perfect. While you may think of beads as all sparkle, wood or bone beads can add ethnic accents, while seed pearls are quite elegant and sophisticated. Many beads can be stitched on with regular sharps and thread, but you may have to use a beading needle and nylon beading thread depending on how teeny your beads are.

Buttons. They're not all work and no play, you know. Though they will keep your bag closed quite contentedly, let buttons have a little fun as a decorative accent. Look for retro buttons, antique mother-of-pearl buttons, or even art-to-wear buttons made by enamelists or silversmiths. Use just one great button, or a grouping.

Stitch on beads for some flash.

Experiment with the various materials and techniques you can use for embellishment.

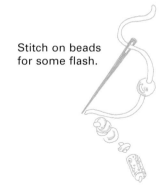

Trims. Shop for trim—cording, piping, ribbon, fringe, lace, braid, tassels—in both the garment and decorator sections of the fabric store. You can make your own fabric trim with a bias tape maker, and boy is it fun. There are some spectacular trims available, embroidered and beaded by hand, that may be more expensive than the fabric you'll buy! But a little funky lime-green rickrack may be just the thing for *your* bag.

Novelty yarns. If you have a good knitting shop nearby, pay it a visit. The over-the-top popularity of knitting has led to some dynamite materials on the market, from cotton cord to variegated silk.

Sequins. For true dazzle, add a sequin (or a couple hundred). And they're not just tiny and round anymore—they're square, oblong, bursting with color, and *big*. Shop for specialty sequins on the Internet.

Tulle. Tulle is not just for tutus. If you want sheer drama, add some tulle as a top layer on your bag, or make trim from lengths of it. Tulle's cousin, netting, has a larger weave.

Eyelets and grommets. Like buttons, grommets and eyelets can be very functional, but they like to have fun too. They can be totally decorative—make a swirl of eyelets or a swoosh of grommets—and installing them is very easy. The pliers are particularly simple to use; just practice a time or two to get the right amount of pressure.

Jewelry. Just like Romeo and Juliet, handbags and jewelry have a real attraction to one another. Add a bracelet as a wrist strap, a necklace as a fashionable handle, or an old brooch as focal piece.

Silk flowers. Absolutely. No more needs to be said.

Techniques

There are some decorative techniques you can use to adorn your handbags too—some that you create with your sewing machine.

Appliqué. The art of applying material to the surface of fabric is used frequently in this book. Because it's ideal, of course. Appliquéd embellishments don't have to be stitched on, although you can really play with sewing thread, silk ribbon, or embroidery floss to add decorative elements. Heck, just use some glue if you want. And your details don't have to be made from fabric—how about laminated paper or wire mesh?

Add eyelets or grommets in the blink of an eye.

Appliqué doesn't have to be stitched; these playful elements are glued in place.

Straight stitch

French knots

Chain stitch

Couching

Play with machine quilting, try ruffles or pleats, or add needlework to lend pizzazz to your handbag.

Embroidery. The art of ornamental needlework is also ideal for decorating a handbag. Did you know that you could embroider with raffia? Or silk ribbon? Experiment with various media; have a selection of needles with large eyes on hand. Computerized sewing machines also embroider (and if you have one, I'm jealous). This is not your grandmother's embroidery, dear. A few basic stitches are shown at the left.

Couching. Couching feels like something between appliqué and embroidery, though technically it is an embroidery technique. Couching is creating a motif with decorative yarn or thread on your handbag, securing the decorative elements in place with a series of small stitches.

These stitches can be as laid-back or as in-your-face as you want. You can also couch by machine, using a zigzag stitch and the wizardry of invisible thread. Or don't—use regular thread if you'd rather the zigzag stitching be visible.

Snazzy sewing machines have special presser feet that allow you to couch with decorative stitches, even adding strings of pearls. Or so I've been told.

Quilting. Here's the first of several effects you can create at your sewing machine. Simple machine quilting can add dimension to your handbag, not to mention a little fluffiness, too. It's fun to follow the lines of stitching on your fabric's design motifs as you quilt. Simply place a layer of batting between your fabric piece and a piece of thin cotton backing fabric (quilters call this *making a sandwich*), pin carefully, and then stitch in place as desired on your machine. Use a complementary or contrasting thread, depending on how zany you're feeling.

Ruffles and pleats. These construction details add style. A simple ruffle is just gathered and stitched into place. Finish the edges of the ruffle if you want…or don't. No rules here. Pleats can really emphasize the glory of your fabric because you get to marvel at it in abundance. Simply make folds in your fabric and stitch them down when you're sewing the seam.

Topstitching and edgestitching. While topstitching can be functional, helping to hold a lining in place, it's also decorative. Technically speaking, topstitching is a line of stitching done on the right side of the fabric, parallel to an edge or a seam. Edgestitching is topstitching done just at the finished edge, about as close as you can get to it. Topstitching with a contrasting thread creates visual pizzazz.

Embellished Bags

How about a quick break to ooh and aah over these divine embellished bags? Remember that you can use these techniques in your handmade bags too. Have all the fun you can possibly have with this book! Let the inspiration begin.

Tickle yourself pink with brilliant feathers jutting off an otherwise unadorned bag. Use feathers and crimp beads available from any craft store. If you don't like the look of full feathers, trim the quill and then peel away the extra fluff. When you're happy with the way your feathers look, take an upholstery needle and drive it through from the exterior of the purse, wherever you want to place the feather. Push the needle until its eye is centered in the fabric and leave it there. Slide a crimp bead onto a quill, and working from the exterior of the purse, push this quill through the needle's eye and into the interior of the purse. Gently remove the upholstery needle by pushing it out through the interior of the purse. Crimp the exterior bead first, then the interior bead, using pliers to secure both the beads snugly against each side of the fabric.

Embellished by Nathalie Mornu

Give a little extra love to a plain piece of canvas. Felt appliqué is a sure thing for perking up an unadorned bag. Cut various shades of felt into playful shapes, such as flowers and rectangles, and then play around with layering them on top of one another. Once you've decided on a design, hold the layers together by sewing on beads with invisible thread. If you want to add a little texture, tie and knot some novelty yarn between the layers of felt. Arrange the appliquéd pieces on the bag and then either sew or glue them on.

Adorned by Susan McBride

Will your Prince Charming arrive when you carry this purse? Explore the glass slipper idea and create a translucent shoe using laminated gift wrap. Hold the template in place with tape and sew onto the bag with invisible thread. Other accents, such as copper wire, a charm, and a strand of pearls, may also be added. No more cooking and cleaning for you, Cinderella. You're off to the ball!

Embellished by Diana Light

Afraid of embroidery? Don't be: This simple broad chain stitch is en-chain-tingly (ha ha!) easy. And there's no pattern to copy. Simply start at the left hand side and work to the right. Let the needle be your guide in curving the stitching line. That's about all there is to it. You need only an embroidery needle, a pair of scissors, and something to stitch with: yarn, perle cotton, raffia, or good-quality faux raffia ribbon. Oh! And of course you need that forlorn bag, desperate for a makeover.

Not into sewing today? Have a little fun with fabric markers to decorate a plain purse. Either draw or trace your favorite design. Practice on a similar fabric first, if you can; certain colors tend to run more than others, for some odd reason. This purse came with a fabric-covered mirror inside that was perfect for a trial run.

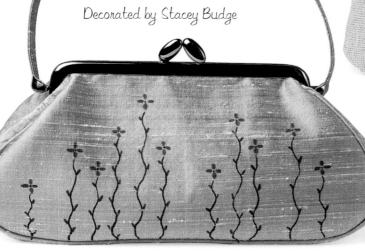

Decorated by Stacey Budge

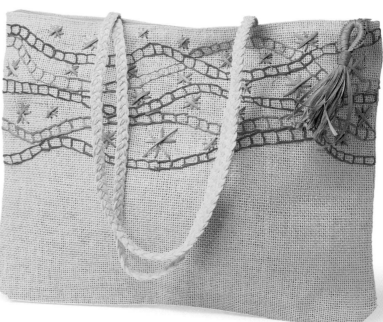

Embellished by Terry Taylor

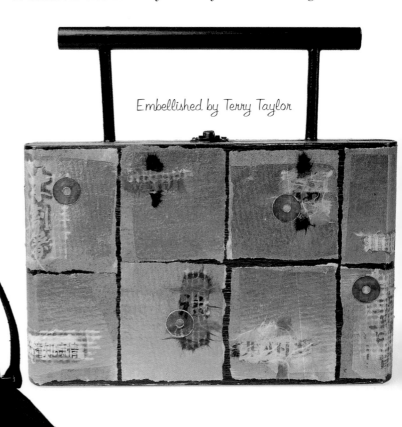

If you and your purse aren't ready for a permanent commitment, try making an interchangeable brooch. You'll need some eye-catching silk flowers in complementary shades, an ice cream stick, beads, a glue gun, and a brooch back (available at craft stores). Remove the plastic centers from the flowers, arrange the petals on the ice cream stick, and glue away. You may want to replace the flower centers with glued or sewn-on beads. Then glue the stick onto the brooch pin. Pin the brooch wherever you like and change it when you're ready for a new look.

Decorated by Susan McBride

Cigar box purses certainly pass the hip test. They present the perfect opportunity to explore many creative techniques: painting, collage, decoupage, beading…even pyrography (woodburning)! But does the thought of puffing on stogies prevent you from creating a cigar box purse? Relax: You can purchase wooden "cigar" boxes at most craft stores these days. While you're there, choose from a wide variety of hardware for it. (Or if you're handy with tools, create your own handles using dowels, a drill, a saw, and wood glue). Then let your imagination run wild with paint, paper, beads, gold leaf, or whatever else strikes your fancy. But no smoking allowed.

Embellished by Terry Taylor

P erhaps you've been holding on to an old belt that just doesn't seem to go with anything anymore, yet you can't part with it. Don't worry—your purse might love it! Position the belt around the middle of the bag. Carefully measure to place three groupings of four eyelet holes around the bag (two groupings in the front of the bag and one on the back). Use a craft knife to mark Xs where the eyelets will be placed. Be sure to put a cutting mat or cardboard inside the purse so you don't cut through the other side of the bag. Add the eyelets, and then use matching leather to lace through them to form a casual belt loop. If you finally do decide to get rid of that belt, you can always spruce up the purse with a fancier one. Or maybe with a bandanna. Or a scarf. Or a chain or a group of necklaces. You get the picture.

N o middle-of-the-road handbag for you. Take a plain brown purse and jazz it up with some funky appliqué. All it takes is varying shades of faux leather (or any other interesting material), some pinking shears, and a little epoxy. Use the pinking shears to cut different-sized shapes from the faux leather. Glue them on top of one another, and then glue them onto your bag. Play with your arrangement before you commit to the glue and allow for plenty of drying time.

Decorated by Megan Kirby

Adorned by Diana Light

A pert paisley pattern will perk up any plain purse. (Say that three times fast!) Buy a stencil, pick your paints, and pounce away with a stencil brush. (Draw and cut your own stencil if you're the DIY type.) Add details to the pattern with the tip of a paintbrush handle. Give the simple rattan handle a coat of matching paint for a polished finish.

Embellished
by Terry Taylor

V intage goes elegant to add a little drama to this handbag. (It's dressed up for the Cannes Film Festival.) Make a rosette from vintage curtains, trimmed with pinking shears. Add a decorative detail such as an old earring. Wrap the purse in tulle, then stitch it to the body of the purse with invisible thread. To hide the raw edges of the tulle, tack on a sparkly trim, also with invisible thread. Sew on the rosette and you're ready for the red carpet.

Adorned by Valerie Shrader

It is obvious that this pocketbook needed an infusion of hipness. And some excitement too. Liven it up with novelty yarns stitched through vintage buttons and old washers. Simply knot and stitch through the buttons and washers beginning on the outside, so the knots and tails show; use embroidery or tapestry needles. (A needle threader is handy when threading these funky yarns) There now— this bag is much happier (and hipper, too).

Embellished by
Valerie Shrader

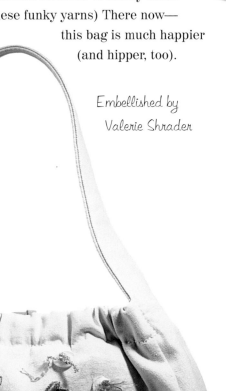

Show off your shape, baby. These popular crocheted bags, often found as rectangles, can easily be accented with similarly shaped objects. In this example, abalone beads mirror the form of the bag and are sewn on with thread that matches the purse. For a little extra sparkle, the abalone beads are then accented with teeny pink pearls, snugly sewn on with beading wire.

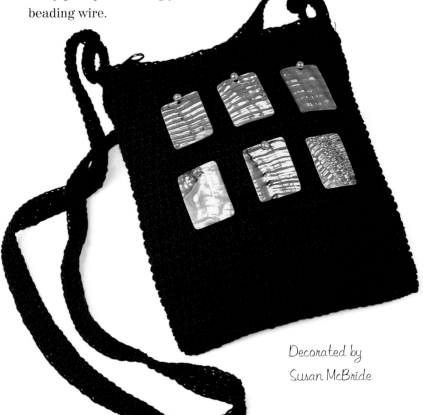

Decorated by
Susan McBride

Take advantage of the pattern on a fabric bag. Bring new life to an interesting design by sewing on your favorite beads, using the existing pattern as a template to guide you. In this example, beads add dimensional pistils, stamens, and stems to the printed flowers. Use beads with contrasting colors, textures, and shapes to emphasize the best parts of the pattern. Simply sew the beads on with invisible thread, being sure to work in a well-lit area.

Embellished by Susan McBride

Engage in urban archeology and search through your belongings to uncover some interesting found objects—a bit of silver chain, an unfinished earring, a luminous button, and some glowing pearls—to complement this fabric collage. Add dimension by covering strips of batting with pieces of silk (these are dupioni swatches) and stitch them onto the purse; let them ravel unabashedly. Add any baubles you've excavated, stitching them on with invisible thread.

Adorned by Valerie Shrader

Prepare to Sew

Okay, the fun is just about to start. But first, let's review the tools and materials you'll need. And let's talk about sewing for *just* a minute. Then on to the hip projects!

Tools and Materials

To make handmade bags, you need a sewing machine, of course, and all of the tools and materials that any sewer has on hand—pins, needles, thread, marking tools, scissors, pinking shears, tape measures, and the like. For either handmade or embellished purchased bags, you'll likely want a wide array of decorative treatments such as beads, sequins, and novelty trims.

Sewing machine. To make the handbags in this book, you don't need a special machine or attachments; about all the machine needs to do is stitch forward, reverse, and zigzag. Well, you might make a few buttonholes, too, come to think of it. Make sure you haven't lost your zipper foot, because you may need that. Before you begin sewing in earnest, check the thread tension using a piece of the fabric you'll be using for your bag.

Of course, you can't sew without good, sharp needles on your machine. Have a range of sizes available and remember to change them often. Every time you hit a pin, you'll need a new needle. Doggone it.

Thread. Gotta have it. Match it to your fabric or choose a color that contrasts if that's the look you're after. Cotton-wrapped polyester should work just fine for your hand-bags. Invisible thread—nylon monofilament—is wonderful for attaching adornments, because it's so very invisi-ble, of course. You can also use it in your sewing machine if you want to.

Pins and needles. This is how you feel when you're ready to cut out your first bag. Kidding. Regular dressmaker's pins are essential to piece your bag together; the newer and sharper, the better. Silk pins—longer and thinner than dressmaker's pins—should be used on light- to medium-weight fabrics.

You'll probably find an assortment of craft needles helpful, depending on the kind of embellishment you're inspired to create. A variety of embroidery needles will probably do the trick. For hand sewing with regular thread, have several sizes of sharps on hand.

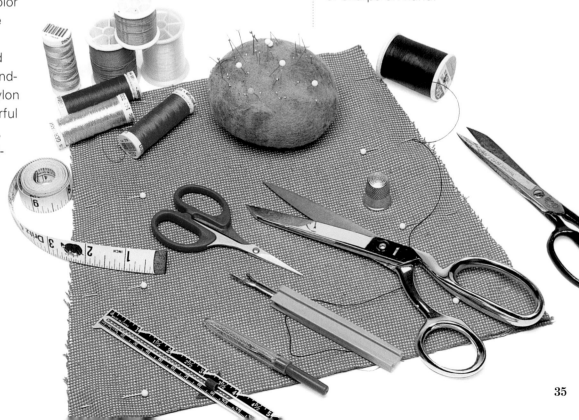

Marking tools. You won't be doing much marking for these patterns, but you will probably use a water-soluble marking pen or dressmaker's pencil at some point. Check the disappearability (no, it's probably not a real word) of the marking pens on a scrap of your fabric. I beg you.

Turning tools. There are some little tools that can really help when you're making a handbag, and one of them is a pointer and creaser, also called a point turner. The tip of this wood or plastic tool pokes out the angles of any piece that needs it, such as the corner of a square flap. When you're shopping, you may find this tool in the quilting section.

You may also want a bodkin or a loop turner to turn a bias strip or strap inside out. My loop turner and I are not on very good terms, but maybe you have a better relationship with yours.

Measuring tools. I've found that I use my hem gauge an awful lot in making handbags because of the scale of the projects. Have a tape measure and a ruler on hand, too.

Bias tape maker. A wonderful gadget that lets you make your own bias tape.

Seam ripper. Oh boy. I hope you use yours less than I use mine. It's such an indispensable tool that I have three, in varying sizes—mishap, mistake, and disaster.

Fabric scissors. A good sharp pair of dressmaker's shears is a necessity; maybe you'll want some pinking shears, too. Embroidery scissors are nice to have for more detailed work.

Clean newsprint or similar paper. To make your patterns from the grids included in this book, you need some thin paper. While there are some fairly long pieces used in the book (I think the largest is about 31 inches long), you can always tape smaller pieces of paper together. An art supply store is a good place to look for pattern-making paper.

Pencils and markers. Have a few around for making and marking the patterns.

Craft scissors. Do not use your fabric scissors on paper. *Verboten!* Use these instead.

Iron and ironing board. Keep the iron plugged in. While it's sometimes difficult to press after every step while handbag sewing, do the best you can. Important: Test every fabric with the iron before you use it on your actual handbag, especially if you've got a remnant and you're unsure of its fiber content. Some fabrics develop a shine when pressed.

If you really get into making handbags, there are some specialized pressing aids that tailors use that will help you reach into the tight spaces and curved areas of a handbag. Pressing hams, pressing mitts, and seam rolls will make it easier to press your bag.

Decorative materials. Well, I'm going to leave this up to you (and your ever-present muse). The materials used as embellishments in this book include embroidery floss, fabric swatches, raffia, tulle, shells, jewelry, feathers, beads, trim, buttons, sequins, rickrack, ribbon, artificial flowers, decorative papers, wire...celebrate the possibilities.

Sewing 101

I'd feel better if we can review some basic sewing terms so we're all on the same page (literally!). Somewhere along the way to handbag nirvana, you'll undoubtedly be instructed to do some of these things.

Baste. Use a line of long stitches to hold pieces in place temporarily.

Clip. Snip into the seam allowance; you definitely want to clip the inward curves of your bag.

Face. Finish a raw edge or a handbag piece with a facing.

Finger press. Some sturdy upholstery fabrics don't press well due to weight or fiber content. And really, sometimes it's difficult to press a handbag because of its inherent design. Finger pressing is useful here: use your fingers to apply pressure to open a seam or push a lining flat.

Hem. In this book, this term usually means finish the edges, as in those of a pocket, by narrowly turning under the raw edges; pressing; turning the edge under again; pressing; and then stitching.

Notch. Cut a notch into the seam allowance; you definitely want to notch the outward curves of your bag.

Pivot. To turn the fabric in another direction while you sew. Lift the presser foot, leaving the needle in the down position, and pivot the fabric. Depending on your fabric choice, it may be helpful to clip the corner of one of the pieces to make the turn easier. Then lower the presser foot and continue.

Press. Did you know there is a difference between pressing and ironing? When you press, you don't move the iron across the fabric—that's ironing. To press means just that—pressing the iron against the fabric. Generally, you should press each seam after you stitch it.

Seam allowance. The amount of fabric between the cut edge and the seamline.

Seamline. The seamline is the stitching line. In this book, it's *always* ½ inch.

Topstitch. Decorative (or functional) stitching on the right side of your handbag.

Trim. Trimming seams is usually a good idea to eliminate bulk. You can also grade the seam allowances, which is to trim one layer shorter than the other.

Turn. In this book, you'll need to turn lots of straps through to the right side. Depending on the material, this can be easy (silk) or not so easy (upholstery fabric). The straps in these projects usually have a seam that you can push against to turn the strap inside out. You can use the pushing or pulling tool that seems to work for you—a bodkin, a loop turner, a chopstick, whatever.

Whipstitch. These are tiny hand stitches you'll use to attach linings; technically speaking, the stitches appear slanted.

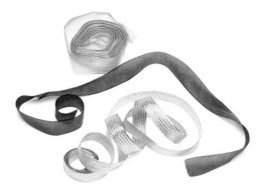

Making Your Pattern

Instead of including actual patterns in this book, we've provided templates on a grid so you can make your own patterns at home, reducing or enlarging them to your heart's content. The scale we've used is 1 square equals 2 inches. Simply create your own grid to these measurements and draw in the pattern pieces. Our patterns *include*, I repeat *include*, the ½ seam allowance, so you don't have to make additional adjustments. After you've drawn the pieces on paper, using the grid system, cut them out with a pair of craft scissors.

If you want the bag smaller, reduce the size of the squares, but keep the proportions (the number of squares in each piece) the same. Want it bigger? Make the squares larger, again keeping the proportions of the pieces the same. (If math is not your thing, here's how you can cheat: Make your pattern pieces the size we've used in the book. Trim off the seam allowances. Then, fiddle with the pattern pieces at a copy machine, *reducing or enlarging each pattern piece the same percentage until you've reached the size you want.* Remember to add the ½ seam allowance to the pieces after you've sized them.)

A template like this is provided for all the seven basic patterns. Make your pattern pieces from these grids; one square equals 2 inches.

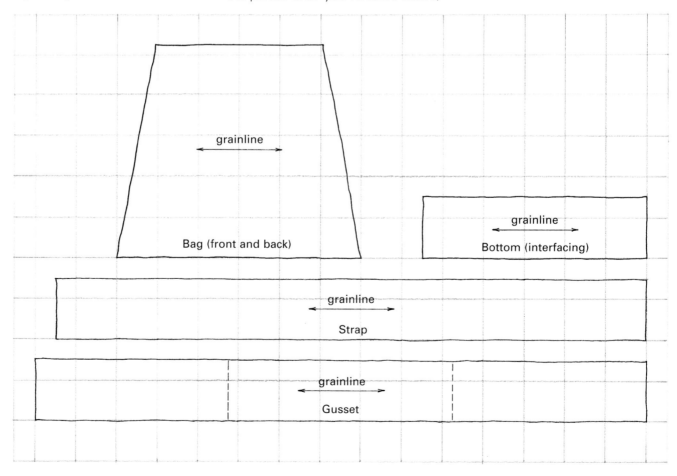

grainline

Bag (front and back)

grainline

Bottom (interfacing)

grainline

Strap

grainline

Gusset

READ ME!
(Please.)

You know when you're installing new software on your computer, there's always that annoying file that screams READ ME? Well, there's one in this book, too. I'm sorry; I know you're ready to sew, but here are some last-minute reminders that will make your hip handbag experience a happy one.

Ask the good folks at your fabric or crafts store for advice if you're unfamiliar with the properties of the fabric that interests you. Tell them what you're doing, and ask if they have any advice about sewing with the fabric you've chosen. Same applies for interfacings, too.

Prewash all your fabrics that can be washed.

Press the fabric before you cut out the pieces for your handbag.

Cut all the pieces on the lengthwise grain if possible; crosswise is okay, too, if the amount of your fabric is limited. If you make your own piping, those pieces should be cut on the bias.

Test dressmaker's pencils or marking pens on a scrap of your fabric.

Check the tension on your machine by using a swatch of your fabric. Make sure you have the needle size right; the needle ought to be good and sharp, too.

Make a practice "mistake." Some materials don't leave you any room for error, for if you stitch a seam and then have to rip it out, the needle holes remain. Bummer. Leather, suede, and novelty nonwoven fabrics (like vinyl) fall into this category. Before you sew, it's a good idea to do a test seam on a scrap and then try to remove it to see how your fabric responds to the oops factor.

Test all your new techniques on a scrap piece of your fabric before you commit to incorporating it into your handbag. I'm talking about things like installing grommets and magnetic clasps as well as decorative techniques such as embroidery or quilting. Just maybe it won't turn out as you hoped, so check it out first. Please.

Work within your comfort zone— if you'd rather baste by hand than by machine, have at it. If you'd rather make your straps differently than what I suggest, feel free. Apply your skills to the projects because, remember, it's all about the fun.

Remember that the seam allowance is **½ inch** for all the patterns.

I realize I've been a little bit of a know-it-all in this part of the book. Why? Well, it's not because I'm so smart—it's because I've already made all these mistakes I've been warning you about. I'm just trying to save you a lot of seam rippin', darling.

Now go have some fun!

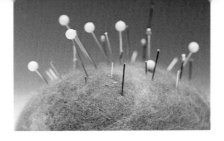

The Sewing Kit

Here are the basic tools and materials that we're going to assume you have on hand to make a handbag. When you see "Sewing Kit" listed in the instructions, these are the things we're talking about. You won't need all of these supplies to embellish a bag, but I suspect you'll certainly need a pair of scissors.

Sewing machine

Thread

Nylon thread, invisible (clear) and dark

Needles (machine and hand)

Thimble

Pins

Pincushion

Marking tools—water-soluble pens or dressmaker's pencils

Turning tools—point turner, bodkin, loop turner

Measuring tools—tape measure, hem gauge, ruler

Seam ripper

Scissors—embroidery scissors and shears

Craft scissors

Clean newsprint or similar paper for making patterns

Pencils and markers

Iron and ironing board

Project Key

Here's the template you'll see for each of the project instructions, followed by a description of the information you'll find under each heading.

• That's the title of the bag, with a catchy sentence or two about it.

The Actress

It tries to be businesslike, but this bag's dreamy silk lining and sophisticated design give it away. It's totally Grace Kelly, movie star.

Hip Index
Slightly Elegant
Bag Pattern
The Flirt

• **HIP INDEX**

Just how hip is this handbag? It might be Slightly Elegant, Totally Elegant, Somewhat Funky, Absolutely Funky, or Somewhere In Between.

• **BAG PATTERN**

All of the projects are based on one of the seven basic patterns presented in the book and the handmade handbag projects are organized by these patterns. Just in case you're thumbing through the book and don't know which section you've wandered into, here's where you'll find which pattern to use to create a specific project. Refer to the pattern instructions that start each section for the basic construction of the project.

• SPECIAL TOOLS OR MATERIALS

In the pattern instructions, you'll learn how much yardage you need for the basic design, as well as any basic tools and materials you'll need to make a handbag from that pattern. But here, in the project instructions, you'll find listed any razzle-dazzle tools or supplies that the designer used to customize the handbag for the project.

• HOW IT'S DIFFERENT

The information under this heading will tell you how the construction of a particular project may vary from the pattern on which it's based. Be sure to read all the way through the instructions for the pattern *and* the project before you start cutting out your handbag. An ounce of prevention is worth a pound of fabric scraps.

• FABRIC

The type of fabric used in the project is listed here—if I figured out what that fabric was. Frankly, some of the fabrics were impossible to categorize because they were remnants from outlets. If it is listed as simply "upholstery fabric," that's as close as I could get. If you see the phrase "decorator" in front of the fabric it means the material is a home décor fabric, not a garment fabric.

If you see a word in **type like this** in the instructions, it's a technique that's explained in the Handbag Basics. Remember to flip back to that section if you need to see the illustrated instructions for any of the techniques.

Special Tools
or Materials

Cord, 1 yard

Specialty yarn, 1 ball

Chenille (embroidery) needle

Fabric

Decorator fabric;
vintage silk lining

How It's Different

It's not! Follow the pattern
instructions for
construction.

How It's Special

Add the couching before you
apply the interfacing to the
front. (Actually, buckram was
used instead of interfacing on
this bag for additional structure.)
Couching is simple—all you do
is stitch the cording in place
using the decorative yarn. Use a
chenille needle with a large eye
so you can thread the variegat

HANDMADE BY
Valerie Shrader

Hot Tip

If you want this bag to be
super-structured, use buckram to interface the front
and back, too.

Cool Alternative

If you want this bag to have a
sleeker silhouette, you may
wish to use satin or silk.

Helpful Hint for Happy Sewing

The bracelet makes it a little more difficult to sew the bag, but all
good things come in time. You just have to manipulate the
bracelet inside the bag as you stitch the sides.

• COOL ALTERNATIVE

You might find some suggestions here about how to play around with a design to make it different.

• HOT TIP

Here's a little extra something about the design.

• HOW IT'S SPECIAL

The information under this heading generally talks about the decorative aspects of the handbag, as opposed to the construction details. Sometimes the line between the two is a little blurry.

• HELPFUL HINT FOR HAPPY SEWING

This is info about the project that just might make your sewing less stressful and thus more fun. And you know this book is all about the fun.

Pattern

Materials & Tools

Fabric, ½ yard

Lining (or second fabric), ½ yard

Fusible interfacing, ½ yard

Cord, 1¼ yards

Sewing kit

Pieces to Cut

Bag—1 of fabric, 1 of lining (or second fabric), and 1 of interfacing

Remember to use ½-inch seam allowances.

Handbag Basics on pages 16–23.

The Messenger

Over the shoulder and off you go. Put on The Messenger, give it an adoring pat, and feel secure that it's right by your side.

How You Make It

1. Apply the interfacing to the wrong side of the fabric piece.

2. Measure 9 inches down from one end of the bag, marking at each side. Pin one end of the cord to each side at the marks, making sure the raw edges are even (figure 2). Pin the fabric piece to the lining, right sides together, with the cord between the two layers and not caught in the seam allowances. Stitch around the bag, leaving a 4-inch section open in the end away from the cord.

3. Turn the bag right side out through the opening and press. Stitch the opening by hand or machine. Fold the bottom up to the cord and press.

4. Stitch the sides in place by hand or machine, sewing very close to the edge.

Cool Alternative

This bag can be completely reversible if you desire,
so choose a hip fabric for the lining, too.

Hot Tip

You can vary where you place the cord and the fold depending on
how long you want the flap to be.

Figure 2

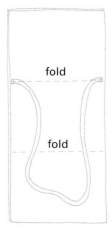

fold

fold

Figure 1

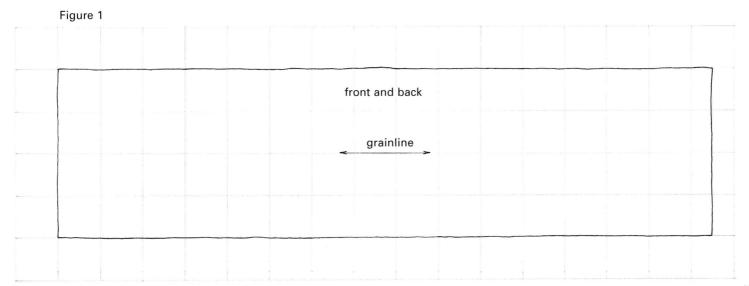

front and back

grainline

1 square = 2 inches

The Lazy River

This bag just flows along, taking you for a leisurely cruise. Don't forget the sunscreen.

Special Tools and Materials

¼-inch piping, 1 yard

¾-inch cording, 1¼ yards

Fabric

Decorator tapestry;
  silk dupioni lining

HANDMADE BY
Joan K. Morris

How It's Different

Just a couple of little things here: add the piping around the flap with a zipper foot. (You probably already know that, but look at **piping** in **Handbag Basics**, page 22, if you need to.) The side seams of this bag were stitched together by hand so it would have no visible seams on either side when you reverse it. Use strong thread and tiny stitches if you decide you want that look for your bag, too.

The Artist

This one's too creative for only one style of adornment; it has to be reversible to display its other talents, too.

Special Tools or Materials

Specialty yarn, 1 ball

Rickrack, 1 spool

Sequin trim, 1 spool

Fabric

Upholstery; upholstery lining

HANDMADE BY
Valerie Shrader

How It's Different

There are a couple of itty-bitty changes here. The first is the fabric strap, constructed like skinny little **Strap B** in the **Handbag Basics** (page 19). It's about 45 inches long. Also, The Artist has been folded so the flap is as long as the bag.

How It's Special

All the accoutrements are added by freeform machine couching, using invisible thread. Just place the trim at the edge of the cut piece and start stitching. Let your muse do the rest!

The Marie Antoinette

This bag is opulent and extravagant just like its namesake, yet far more gracious.

Special Tools or Materials

Upholstery trim, ¼ yard

Cording, ¾ yard

Fabric

Decorator brocade; brocade lining

How It's Different

This bag is a scaled-down version of The Messenger, the bag pattern piece reduced to about 9 x 22 inches. Leave the *flap* end open when you stitch the fabric and lining together.

How It's Special

Fold under the raw edges of the flap; sandwich the trim between the two layers. Baste in place by hand. Fold the bottom edge as desired, but don't stitch the sides just yet. Now, decide how long you want the strap, remembering to figure in the length of the sides of the bag, and cut the cording. Sandwich the flange of the cording between the two folded layers of fabric. Stitch the sides and use a small pair of scissors to remove the exposed flange along the handle.

HANDMADE BY
Allison Chandler Smith

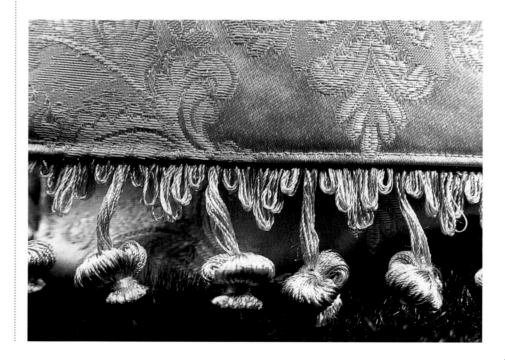

The Spring Day

Oh, flowers in bloom, children at play.
This is one happy bag!

Special Tools or Materials

Handles with screw-in bar

Fabric

Decorator sateen; decorator cotton lining

How It's Different

This bag is based on The Messenger, as the main pattern piece is just one large rectangle, roughly 13 x 20 inches. Cut one large rectangle from each of the coordinating fabrics. Fold the fabric piece in half with right sides together and stitch the sides *except for the top 2 inches*. Turn right side out and press, pressing under the raw edges of the side seams. Repeat this step for the lining.

Fold the top edges of the bag under ½ inch and press; do the same for the lining. Push the lining inside the handbag, wrong sides together, and pin along the top edges. Create a casing at the top by stitching ¼ inch from the edge and again ¾ inch from the edge. If desired, tack the bag and lining together at the sides at the top of the seam. Slip the handles into the casing.

Cool Alternative

If you were feeling a little less like spring and more like summer, you could reverse this bag to display the fabric used in The Summer Day (page 62). Cool, huh?

The Summer of Love Pouch

Hip Index
Somewhat Funky

Bag Pattern
The Messenger

Still as hip now as in 1967, this handbag just wants somebody to love: you, baby.

Special Tools and Materials

Two 1-inch grommets and grommet setter

Leather punch

Tapestry needle

Waxed thread

Fabric

Suede

How It's Different

Let the sewing machine take a break and stitch this one together by hand. (They would've done it that way in Haight-Ashbury, man.)

Use the pattern piece to cut one piece of suede (this handbag doesn't need to be lined), but add 3 inches to the length to accommodate the grommets. With the right sides together, use the leather punch to make holes in the suede. Use the tapestry needle and the waxed thread to sew the seams.

Line up the bottom edge of the flap with the bottom edge of the handbag and install the grommets at the top, 1 inch from each corner of the bag. Cut three strips of suede to desired length for the strap and braid them together. Thread the strap through the grommets and knot. Feeling groovy yet?

HANDMADE BY
Stacey Budge

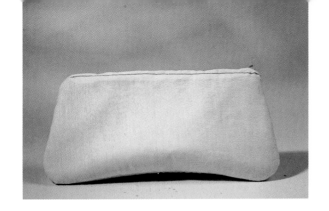

Pattern

Materials & Tools

Fabric, ¼ yard

Lining, ¼ yard

2 pieces of felt, 9 x 12 inches

Zipper, 9 inches

Sewing kit

Pieces to Cut

Bag—2 of fabric, 2 of lining, 2 of felt (for interfacing)

Remember to use ½-inch seam allowances.

Handbag Basics on pages 16–23.

The Clutch

This bag will never leave you, for it likes to be held close. It's just big enough to hold life's essentials—keys, cash, and lipstick.

How You Make It

1. Place the fabric pieces right sides together and pin in place along the top edge. You'll be inserting a **zipper** as in the **Handbag Basics**, but stitch ½ inch from each end instead of 1 inch.

2. Press the seam open, turning the raw edges under. Place the zipper under the pressed edges and pin in place. With a zipper foot, begin stitching at the top of the zipper and continue down one side until you reach the bottom. Lift the zipper foot, leaving the needle in the down position, and pivot the fabric. Lower the zipper foot and stitch across the bottom. Pivot again, stitch back up the other side of the zipper, pivot, and stitch across the top. Make sure the zipper runs freely.

3. To give your bag some nice squeezable support, add the felt interfacing to the wrong side of the bag pieces. Trim ½ inch off the top of each of the felt pieces that you cut out so the top edges of the felt pieces fall just at the edge of the zipper. Whipstitch the top of the felt to the edge of the zipper tape. Baste the sides and bottom of the felt to the inside of the bag, stitching as close as possible to the edge (figure 2).

Figure 1

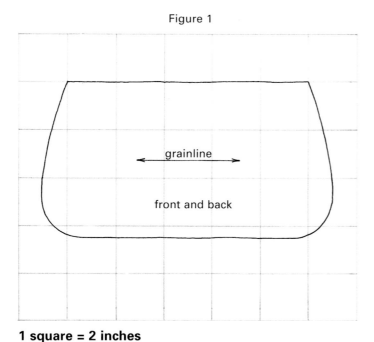

grainline

front and back

1 square = 2 inches

Figure 2

Figure 3

4. Open the zipper about 1 inch. (If you've decided to add a strap, now is the time to pin it in place at the corner [or corners], the raw edges even with the raw edges of the side seams of the bag. Be sure the strap is between the layers and be careful not to catch it in the seams as you sew). Take the handbag, place the right sides together, and pin in place. Stitch all the way around the sides and bottom of the bag (figure 3). Trim the seams and clip the corners. Fully open the zipper and turn the bag right side out.

5. Take the lining pieces and place them right sides together; pin in place. Stitch around the sides and bottom but leave the top edge open, stitching in only ½ inch from each edge. Clip the curves. (This is **Lining B** in the **Handbag Basics**.)

6. Turn under the seam allowance on the open portion of the lining and press. Leave the lining wrong side out. Place it inside the bag, matching the edges. Whipstitch the pressed edge of the lining to the zipper tape, hiding the stitches as much as possible.

The Jewel

This dazzling handbag is adorned with its own necklace. Its flap beckons, "Open me."

Special Tools or Materials

Necklace, 30 inches

Fabric

Silk; satin lining

How It's Different

Make a separate pattern piece for the back that includes the asymmetrical flap, based on The Clutch pattern; use the template in figure 1. Cut out a lining for the flap from the silk, using just the flap portion of the back piece as indicated. After lining the pieces with felt as described in The Clutch instructions (page 54), stitch the flap lining to the flap around the top edges, right sides together. Now stitch the front and the back of the clutch together, right side together. Turn under the raw edge of the flap lining and press. Turn the bag right side out.

Make the clutch lining and leave it inside out. Place the top edge against the front of the bag. Take the edge on the outside, facing you, and pin it to the top edge of the bag, moving the edge closest to the bag out of the way. The right sides should be together. Stitch across the front of the bag only, stopping at the side seams. Turn the lining into the bag. Press the front edge.

HANDMADE BY
Joan K. Morris

Figure 1

Make the flap lining by cutting a pattern piece along the dashed lines.

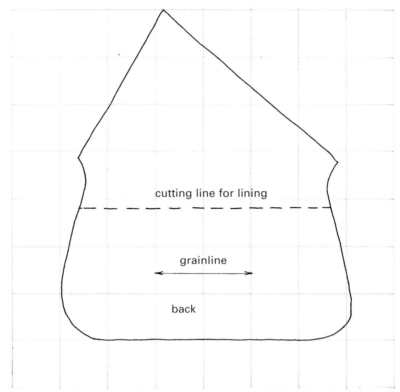

cutting line for lining

grainline

back

1 square = 2 inches

Place the necklace across the back of the bag where the flap meets the bag, putting it under the clutch lining. Stitch the lining in place by hand. Be sure and stitch well where the necklace emerges from the lining to hold it securely in place. Fold the raw edge of the flap lining over the clutch lining. Whipstitch in place.

The Accessory

It's more than a handbag, and more than a bracelet—it's haute couture. And it knows it, too.

Special Tools or Materials

Bracelet

Fabric

Embroidered silk taffeta; satin lining

How It's Different

This clutch has a 1-inch line of stitching at either side of the zipper instead of ½ inch as indicated in The Clutch instructions. The 9-inch zipper was shortened to fit into this opening.

How It's Special

To add the bracelet handle to the bag, make a piece like **Strap B** from the **Handbag Basics** (page 19); the one in this project was cut to 2 x 4 inches, but the size could vary depending on the width of your bracelet. Fold the fabric handle around the bracelet and stitch to encase the bracelet.

Add the bracelet handle before you install the zipper. Pin it ½ inch from the side at the top edge, raw edges together. Stitch it to the clutch as you sew the 1-inch line of stitching to begin installing the zipper.

Helpful Hint for Happy Sewing

The bracelet makes it a little more difficult to sew the bag, but all good things come in time. You just have to manipulate the bracelet inside the bag as you stitch the sides.

HANDMADE BY
Joan K. Morris

59

The Swinger

Dangle this little number off your wrist and the martinis are sure to flow.

Special Tools or Materials

Nonstick presser foot, tissue paper, or tearaway stabilizer

Thin batting

Zipper, 7 inches

¼ inch grommet and grommet setting tool

Swivel hook

Fabric

Synthetic snakeskin; rayon lining

How It's Different

This bag has been scaled down slightly (about 1 inch all around) from the original pattern. Divide the pattern piece for the bag's front into three **panels** for visual interest (page 22); topstitch along each seam. Use a 7-inch zipper. Install the grommet after completing the bag.

Since this fabric won't ravel, you can make a simple strap by merely turning under the raw edges and stitching into place. Attach the strap to a swivel hook secured in place by hand stitches. Oh! Instead of felt, this clutch has a layer of thin batting between the lining and the bag for extra squeezability. And it features a pocket inside. You've got to store life's little treasures somewhere.

Helpful Hint for Happy Sewing #1

This synthetic fabric is much easier to sew if you have a nonstick presser foot. Repeat: This synthetic fabric is much easier to sew if you have a nonstick presser foot. Got it? If you don't have one, you can use tissue paper or tearaway stabilizer to keep the fabric moving under your presser foot. Faux snakeskin has a stubborn streak, but it's fun nonetheless.

Helpful Hint for Happy Sewing #2

When you divide your pattern pieces into panels, remember to account for the seam allowances when you cut out the pieces. The person who made this clutch just may have forgotten to do that and was forced to cut out another piece. Boo hoo.

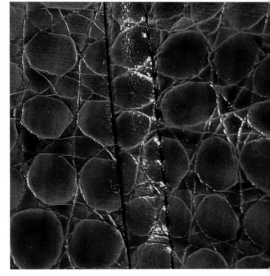

HANDMADE BY
Valerie Shrader

The Summer Day

Oh, picnics and sunshine. The Summer Day is totally reversible and totally fun.

Special Tools or Materials

Fusible interfacing, ¼ yard

Fabric

Decorator cotton; decorator sateen lining

How It's Different

Choose two complementary fabrics to use for this clutch; since it's reversible, either fabric could be the lining or the exterior, to suit your whim. To make it easy, let's call one the fabric (the exterior) and one the lining (inside). Cut out three clutch pieces from both the fabric and the lining (six in all), and three clutch pieces from fusible interfacing. Apply the interfacing to the wrong side of all three pieces cut from the fabric.

Make the front flap by sewing one piece of the fabric to one piece of the lining, right sides together, leaving the top edge open. Turn and press. With right sides together, sew the remaining two lining pieces together, leaving the top edge open. Turn and press. Repeat to make the body of the clutch from the remaining two fabric pieces. Turn and press.

Okay, now concentrate. To assemble the clutch, stack all three sewn pieces together like so: on the bottom, the body of the clutch, back facing up; in the middle, the flap of the clutch with the lining side facing up; and on top, the lining of the clutch. Pin together the three pieces along the top, leaving the bottommost layer of fabric and the topmost layer of fabric free. Stitch through the pinned layers *only*, as shown in figure 1. Push the lining into the bag and press flat. Turn the raw edges under and whipstich the lining to the front of the bag.

Figure 1

Cool Alternative

If you were feeling a little less like summer and more like spring, you could reverse this bag to display the fabric used in The Spring Day (page 50). Clever, huh?

HANDMADE BY
Allison Chandler Smith

The Tote

This friendly all-purpose bag is basic in the best sense of the word; it has everything you want, and nothing you don't. Take it everywhere!

Pattern

Materials & Tools

Fabric, ½ yard

Lining, ½ yard

Buckram, ¼ yard

Fusible interfacing, ½ yard

Sewing kit

Pieces to Cut

Bag—2 of fabric, 2 of lining, 2 of interfacing

Bottom—1 of fabric, 1 of lining, 1 of buckram

Handles—2 of fabric, each 3 x 13 inches; 2 of interfacing, each 3 x 13 inches

Remember to use ½-inch seam allowances.

Handbag Basics on pages 16–23.

How You Make It

1. Apply the fusible interfacing to the wrong sides of the fabric bag pieces. With right sides together, pin the bag pieces together along the sides. Stitch the seams and press them open.

2. Baste the buckram to the wrong side of the fabric bottom piece at the seamline and trim the buckram close to the seamline. Find the center of the bottom by folding the piece lengthwise; mark the centerline at both side edges.

3. With right sides together, pin the fabric bottom piece to the bag, matching the centerline marks on the bottom to the side seams of the bag (figure 2). Stitch the seam, easing the fullness in the bag as necessary. (You may find it easier to pin just the first few inches and then ease the bag onto the curve of the bottom piece as you sew.) Trim the seams and clip the curves. Press the seams to the bottom and turn the bag right side out.

4. Make **Strap A** in the **Handbag Basics.** Apply the interfacing to the wrong sides of the handles; fold one handle piece lengthwise, right sides together. Stitch the length of the handle, pivot, and stitch across one end. Repeat for the second handle. Turn the handles inside out through the open end. Now that you've turned the handles, trim the seam from the short ends so each strap has two open ends with raw edges. Press both pieces flat with the seam in the center.

5. Pin the handles to the bag, right sides together, each end of the strap about 3½ inches from the side seam. (You'll be looking at the seam in the handles if you've got it right.)

Figure 1

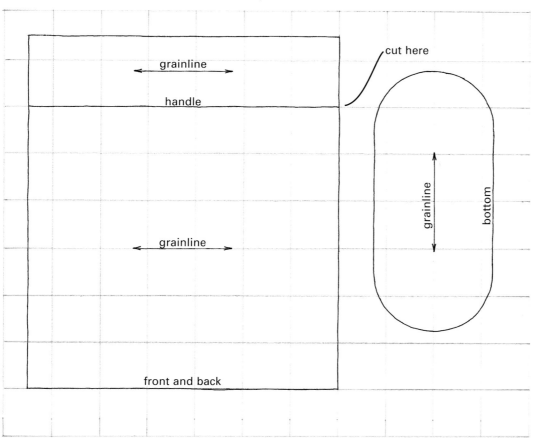

grainline

handle

cut here

grainline

bottom

grainline

front and back

1 square = 2 inches

6. Stitch the lining bag pieces together and then stitch the lining bottom to the bag, as in steps 1 through 3, *but leave 5 inches open in the bottom seam*. Trim the seams and press them open. Leave the lining wrong side out. (This is **Lining A** in the **Handbag Basics** if you want to take a look at it.)

7. With right sides together, place the lining over the bag and align the top edges. Pin the bag to the lining, making sure the handles are lying flat between the fabric and the lining and not somehow caught in the seam allowance. Match the side seams. Stitch and clip the curves.

8. Pull the bag right side out through the 5-inch hole in the lining. Stitch the opening closed by hand or machine. Push the lining into the bag and press the top edge. Topstitch if you want to.

Figure 2

Cool Alternative

Instead of inserting the oval bottom piece, you can also make a simple tote from just two pieces of fabric. Lengthen the front and back piece in this pattern by about 3 inches. Stitch the bag together around the sides and the bottom. Then, with right sides together, fold the bottom corners so the seams meet and stitch across them (figure 3). *Voila!* You've created the bottom from this nifty little seam. To finish, add the handles and lining as described above.

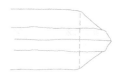

Figure 3

The Polka Dot

Hip Index

Somewhat Funky

Bag Pattern

The Tote

Does this bag want to be noticed, or what? And to think it's reversible, too. What a showoff.

Special Tools or Materials

Handles

1-inch velvet ribbon, ¼ yard, cut
into 4 pieces that are about
2 inches long

Fabric

Reversible decorator cotton
(bag and lining)

How It's Different

This is really cool fabric. Because it's reversible, with two layers of fabric joined together at the polka dots, turn it over to cut the lining pieces after you've cut the bag pieces. Make **lined pockets** as in the **Handbag Basics** (page 20) and stitch them on before you construct the bag; use the reverse side of the fabric to make the pockets for each side (bag or lining, depending on your mood).

The Polka Dot also features shiny handles that are attached with yummy velvet ribbon loops; add them (loops and handles) before the lining is sewn in. A line of stitching across each loop keeps the handle snugly in place.

HANDMADE BY
Joan K. Morris

The Geisha

Hip Index
Slightly Elegant

Bag Pattern
The Tote

There is an air of mystery to this bag.
Don't you wonder what's inside?

Special Tools
or Materials

Chopsticks

Fabric

Silk-faced brocade

How It's Different

This bag is not lined. To accommodate the chopstick handles, make a 4 x 1½–inch cutout in the center of the top of both bag pieces. Clip the inside corners of each cutout to about ¼ inch so you can make a narrow machine hem to finish the raw edges. Assemble the bag as instructed in The Tote, stitching the cutout as you hem the top edge. Sew the chopstick handles across the cutouts by hand.

HANDMADE BY
Stacey Budge

The Parisienne

Ooh la la! Such artistry can only be found in something trés francaise.

Special Tools or Materials

Round faux tortoiseshell handles

Decorative trim(s), ½ yard

Fabric

Decorator brocade; decorator jacquard lining

How It's Different

This is a scaled-down version of The Tote; its finished size is about 9½ x 10 inches (excluding the handles). The pattern piece was altered as shown in figure 1.

After you've made the lining, insert it into the bag, wrong sides together. Turn the raw edges under and pin together along the slanted side edges. Stitch. Fold the top over the handle, folding under the raw edge, and stitch in place by hand. Repeat for the remaining handle.

How It's Special

Cut the decorative trim (this bag has two, the tassles and the fringe) to fit the finished dimensions of the bag. Use a needle and thread to stitch them onto the front and back of the bag.

Figure 1

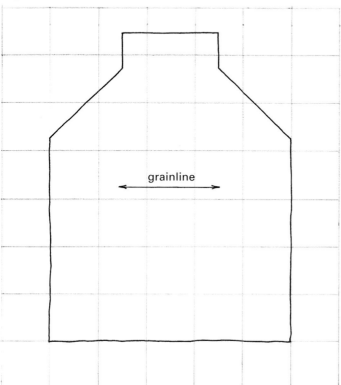

grainline

1 square = 2 inches

HANDMADE BY
Allison Chandler Smith

The Flight of Fancy

Hip Index

Slightly Elegant

Bag Pattern

The Tote

Special Tools and Materials

Silk organza, 1/8 yard, cut into 24 squares that are 2 x 2 inches and 24 squares that are 1½ x 1½ inches

1¾-inch grosgrain ribbon, 1½ yards, cut into 2 pieces that are each 26 inches long

Hair canvas

Fabric

Polyester taffeta; silk organza accents; cotton lining

HANDMADE BY
Nathalie Mornu

How It's Different

Use hair canvas for the interfacing of this handbag. When you stitch the seams, be careful not to catch the organza squares.

Instead of handles, use lengths of grosgrain ribbon. Pin them into place before you line the purse. Place the lining inside the bag, wrong sides together, with the lining's edge a little lower than the handbag's edge. The lining is topstitched in place. Or, you can add the lining as described in the instructions for The Tote. Take your pick.

How It's Special

Embellish the front of the bag before you construct it. Cut out the organza squares, leaving the edges unfinished. Center a smaller square on a larger one and place each pair on the front of the bag in a diagonal orientation. This bag has three evenly spaced rows of four squares each. Pin the pairs of organza squares in place and stitch them to the front.

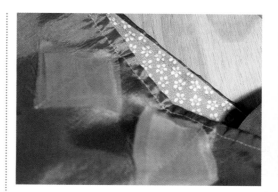

Hot Tip

Use contrasting thread for a little kick—actually, for a *lot* of kick.

Materials & Tools

Fabric, ½ yard

Lining, ½ yard

Buckram, ¼ yard

Fusible interfacing, ½ yard

Sewing kit

Pieces to Cut

Bag—2 of fabric, 2 of lining, 2 of interfacing

Strap—2 of fabric, 1 of interfacing (optional)

Gusset—1 of fabric, 1 of lining, 1 of interfacing

Bottom—1 of buckram

Remember to use ½-inch seam allowances.

Handbag Basics on pages 16–23.

The Tuck

The tidy Tuck fits just under your arm or hugs your side; it loves you! And you'll love it, too, through thick and thin.

How You Make It

1. Mark the dashed lines on the gusset (this is the bottom of the bag). Trim the seam allowances from the buckram and place it in the center of the gusset between the marked lines. Apply the interfacing to the gusset, sandwiching the buckram between the fabric and the interfacing. Apply the interfacing to the wrong sides of the fabric bag pieces.

2. Pin one of the fabric bag pieces to the gusset, right sides together (figure 2). Stitch in place, starting at the top, and continue to within ½ inch of the corner; pivot and stitch to the next corner. (It may be helpful to clip the corner of the gusset to make the turn easier.) Pivot and stitch to the top. Stitch the gusset to the remaining bag piece.

3. Trim the corners. Press the seams open and turn the bag right side out.

4. Make the strap using a slight variation of **Strap A** in **Handbag Basics**. Place the strap pieces right sides together and pin. (For extra strength, add interfacing to one of the strap pieces.) Stitch the two long sides together, leaving the ends open; because this strap is fairly wide, it's easy to turn inside out through one of the ends. Turn and press.

5. Pin one end of the strap to the gusset, right sides together, and stitch in place. Making sure the strap is not twisted, pin and stitch the other end of the strap to the gusset on the other side of the bag.

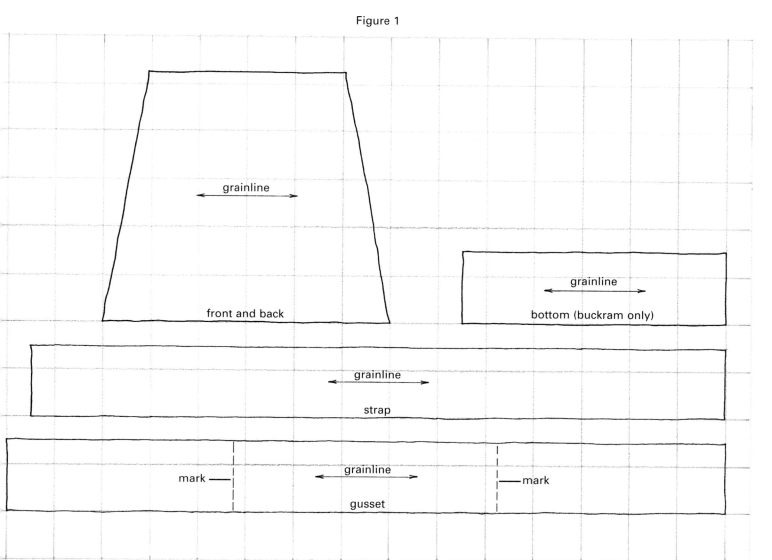

Figure 1

grainline

front and back

grainline

bottom (buckram only)

grainline

strap

mark

grainline

mark

gusset

1 square = 2 inches

6. Make the lining as in step 2, *leaving a 5-inch opening in one of the bottom seams*. Press the seams open. (Look at **Lining A** in the **Handbag Basics** if you want to take a peek at the illustrations for this method.) Leave the lining wrong side out.

7. Place the lining over the bag, so the right sides of the bag and the lining are together. Be sure the strap is situated properly between the bag and the lining. Pin the raw edges of the lining and the bag together, matching the side seams. Stitch all the way around the top. Trim the seams and clip the curves.

8. Turn the bag right side out through the 5-inch hole in the bottom of the lining. Stitch the opening closed by hand or machine. Push the lining into the bag and press the top edge. Topstitch if desired.

Figure 2

Hot Tip

If you want a really stiff bag, use buckram (½ yard) instead of fusible interfacing. Then you can omit the buckram insert in the gusset.

The Cosmos

This bag comes from a candy-coated universe where everyone is in the pink, and you will be too when you're carrying this cosmic confection.

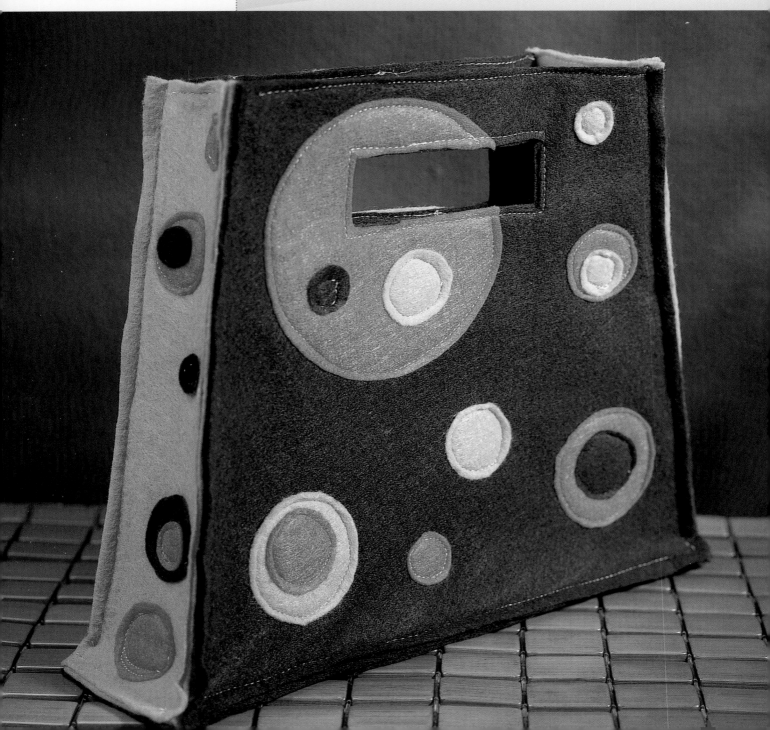

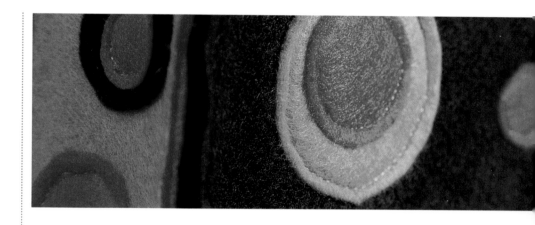

Special Tools and Materials

Buckram, ½ yard

Fabric

Felt

How It's Different

You won't be adding the strap to this variation of The Tuck. Instead, cut a space into the bag pieces for the handle. Divide the gusset into two pieces, one for the sides and one for the bottom; remember to add the seam allowance to the new pieces. Since The Cosmos is lined with felt, cut out four bag pieces, four side pieces, and two bottom pieces.

From the buckram, cut one front, one back, two side pieces, and one bottom piece. Trim away an additional ⅜ inch from all the buckram edges, including those around the handle areas. Now the buckram won't peek through after the bag is stitched.

HANDMADE BY
Nathalie Mornu

For each piece, sandwich the buckram between the two layers of felt and pin together. Cut out felt circles in a variety of sizes. Arrange as desired and pin. Topstitch in place. Then topstitch around the handles. The sides with appliqués on them will be the exterior of the purse. Assemble the pieces with wrong sides facing and pin, beginning with the sides. Stitch with the seams on the outside. Then sew the bottom to the bag. Topstitch along the top of the bag and trim any seams if desired.

How It's Special

Appliqué is an easy way to add some life to the surface of your handbag. These felt appliqués are easily stitched on by machine.

Helpful Hint for Happy Sewing #1

Because felt doesn't ravel, you don't have to finish the raw edges and you can leave the seams exposed.

Helpful Hint for Happy Sewing #2

Adding the cosmic appliqués after you've assembled the felt "sandwich" helps keep the pieces together. But you might find it a little easier to put the appliqués on before you assemble the sandwiches, as you'll be working with fewer layers of felt.

The Curlicue

Hip Index
Somewhere in Between

Bag Pattern
The Tuck

The Curlicue just wants to have fun, with straps going every which a way and quilting that follows the swirling pattern of the fabric.

Special Tools or Materials

Lightweight batting

Lightweight cotton, ¼ yard

2 large O or D rings

Magnetic clasp

Fabric

Upholstery; contrasting upholstery trim; cotton lining

How It's Different

The Curlicue's flap is faced with the lining material; the flap's finished size is about 2½ x 4½ inches. Install one half of the magnetic snap on the flap, with the other placed on the bag itself. Construct the **flap** and add it to the bag, as suggested in the **Handbag Basics** (page 21), before you add the lining. Remember to put the other side of the magnetic snap on the bag before you line it, too. The lining also has a simple **unlined pocket** like the one in **Handbag Basics** (page 21).

Divide the strap into three parts, each faced with the contrasting fabric. Arrange the strap pieces so the middle piece has different fabric on the outside than the other two. Finish the raw edges of the straps, wrap them around the rings, and stitch into place. Add the strap according to instructions for The Tuck.

How It's Special

There's some subtle machine quilting on the front of The Curlicue that offers just a bit of dimension. It's very simple machine quilting: Apply the interfacing to the wrong side of the front fabric bag piece. Place the front wrong side up and add a layer of batting cut to the same shape. Then place a piece of thin cotton on top, also cut to the same shape of the bag. Carefully pin the layers together, turn, and stitch along the designs using a long stitch. You could also stitch it by hand and use contrasting thread or embroidery floss, if the spirit moved you.

HANDMADE BY
Valerie Shrader

Helpful Hint for Happy Sewing

These magnetic clasps hold tight. I mean *really* tight. And the skimpy little directions that come with the clasps do not enlighten you to this fact. If you use them, be sure that you've added lots of sturdy interfacing, maybe even buckram, underneath both parts of the clasp so you can pull the thing apart without tearing it out of your fabric.

The Petite Purse

So much luxury in such a small handbag.
This one demands a night on the town with you.

Special Tools or Materials

None

Fabric

Silk matka; silk dupioni panels and lining

How It's Different

This is a small, adorable version of The Tuck, only about 5 x 7½ inches when all is said and done. Panels have been created in the bag and the gusset pieces, but they differ a little from the method described in **Handbag Basics** (page 22). Create the panels in your pattern, remembering to add the ½ seam allowance. For the middle section, cut the fabric three times as long as the pattern piece and gather it to fit.

Instead of sewing the panels together right sides facing, turn under a ½-inch hem on the bag panels. Pin the gathered panel under these hemmed edges, right side of the gathered panel to the wrong side of the bag panels. Topstitch in place.

HANDMADE BY
Nathalie Mornu

How It's Special

Before you stitch the gusset to the bag (and way before you add the lining), create the fabric closure. Use **Strap B** from **Handbag Basics** (page 19) to create a length of skinny dupioni ribbon; when it's finished, it should be about 30 inches long and about ⅜ inch wide. With plenty of length on each side, tie three or four knots in the ribbon, making a frog. Cut the ribbon to the height of the bag, making sure the knot will fall in the middle of the gathered panel. Stitch in place on the front at the top and the bottom.

With the remaining ribbon, make a loop at one end to fit the knot and stitch the loop in place. Cut this ribbon to the length necessary to close the bag when the ribbon is sewn in the bottom seam at the back of the bag. Stitch it in place before you add the gusset.

The Best in Show

Primp and fluff and prance and shine.
This one's pedigree is obvious.

Special Tools or Materials

⅞-inch sequins, approximately 160

Embroidery floss

Embroidery needle

Handles

Grosgrain ribbon, narrow enough to fit through the holes in the handles

Piping, ¾ yard

Fabric

Decorator cotton twill; lamé lining

How It's Different

Divide the pattern pieces to create **panels** as described in the **Handbag Basics** (page 22), remembering to add the seam allowances to each panel. The finished size of each panel is 1½ inches wide.

To see if you want this same arrangement for your handbag, play around with the sequins on the pattern before you begin to cut. Remember to account for the length of floss from which the glittery sequins will dangle.

After you've cut out the panels (remember those seam allowances I just talked about) and stitched them together, measure and mark where the sequins will hang. Add the sequins (see How It's Special) before you construct the purse.

Pin the piping to the top edge of the handbag before you add the lining. Also, add the handles using ribbon loops, which should be pinned in place before the lining is added.

How It's Special

Use three strands of embroidery floss to sew on the sequins. Insert the needle from the back at the marked spots. Place three sequins on the floss and push the needle back into the seam at precisely the same place you poked it through. Let the sequins hang from a length of floss. Repeat for all the sequins, making sure they all hang the same distance below the seams.

Helpful Hint for Happy Sewing

You'll need more fabric than is suggested in The Tuck pattern instructions; 1 yard ought to do it.

Hot Tip

This embellishment was designed to hang from the seams so the handbag has a crisp, precise structure. Since the sequins fall below the seam on a strand of embroidery floss, rather than being stitched tightly to the bag, they shimmy with the movement of the purse (and with yours, too).

HANDMADE BY
Nathalie Mornu

The Natural Beauty

The luminous raw silk, decorated by block printing, is all the refinement that this comely bag needs.

Special Tools or Materials

Textile paint

Carved blocks or found objects

Fabric

Raw silk; silk Honan lining

How It's Different

It's not! Follow the pattern instructions for construction.

HANDMADE BY
Barbara Zaretsky

How It's Special

Apply any surface decoration techniques, such as the block printing here, on the cut pieces before construction begins. You can use purchased stamps to create your own designs, but you can be really creative using found objects, too, such as jar lids, the edges of a ruler, or the precut wood shapes from a craft store. Be sure to use paint designed for textiles.

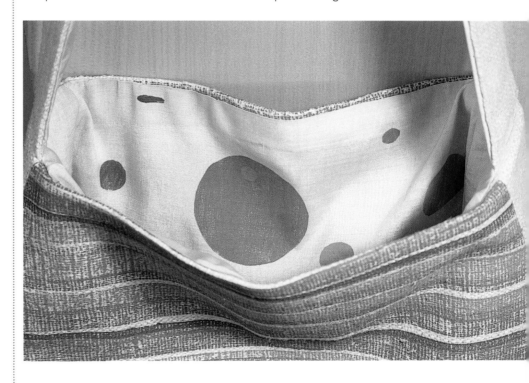

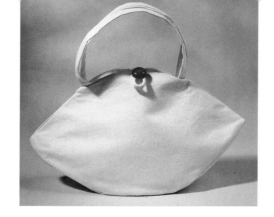

Materials & Tools

Fabric, ½ yard

Lining, ½ yard

Buckram, ¼ yard

Fusible interfacing, ½ yard

Button

Button-and-carpet thread

Sewing kit

Pieces to Cut

Bag—2 of fabric, 2 of lining, 2 of interfacing

Bottom—1 of fabric, 1 of lining, 1 of buckram

Handles—2 of fabric, each 2 x 13 inches; 2 of interfacing, each 2 x 13 inches

Remember to use ½-inch seam allowances.

Handbag Basics on pages 16–23.

The Flirt

Can't you just see this bag giving a sly wink? The Flirt is a perky design that can go elegant or edgy—just like you.

How You Make It

1. Apply the interfacing to the wrong side of the fabric bag pieces and the fabric handle pieces. Baste the buckram to the wrong side of the fabric bottom piece at the seamline and trim the buckram close to the seamline.

2. Pin the bottom to one of the bag pieces, starting at the ½-inch seamline. You'll need to ease the two pieces together; it's probably easier to pin the first section of the seam and then ease around the curves as you sew. Stitch, beginning and ending the seam at the ½-inch seamline. Repeat this step to sew the bottom to the other bag piece. Trim the seams and clip the curves.

3. Measure and mark 4 inches from the seamline at each corner. Stitch from the corners to the marks, leaving an 8-inch opening (figure 2). Turn the handbag right side out and press as best you can.

4. To make the handles, fold the fabric pieces in half lengthwise and press. Now, fold the raw edges into the center, fold in half, and press. Stitch as close to the edge as you can. (You remember—this is **Strap B** in the **Handbag Basics**.)

5. Place the handles in position on the outside of the bag, with the raw edges up at the seamline and the handles flat on the bag (figure 3). Stitch them in place on both sides.

6. To make the button closure, make a skinny little **loop** as described in the **Handbag Basics** (**Strap B** again)—cut the fabric piece about 1 x 4½ inches. Place it at the center of the opening in the back of the handbag, raw edges at the seamline. Stitch in place.

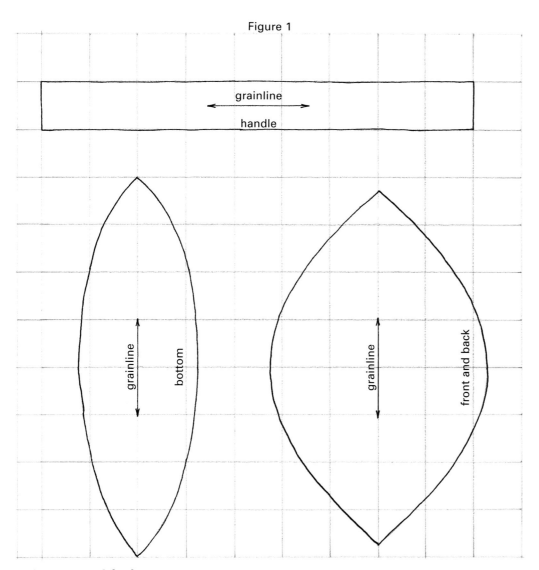

Figure 1

grainline

handle

grainline

bottom

grainline

front and back

1 square = 2 inches

7. For the lining, repeat steps 2 and 3, *but leave 5 inches open in one of the bottom seams*. (Yes, this is **Lining A** from the **Handbag Basics**.) Leave the lining wrong side out. Slip the lining over the bag, right sides together, and pin. Stitch.

8. Pull the bag through the 5-inch opening in the lining. Stitch the opening closed by hand or machine. Push the lining inside the bag and press the top edge. Sew the button in place on the front of the bag; use button-and-carpet thread for extra security.

Hot Tip

If you want this bag to be super-structured, use buckram (½ yard) to interface the front and the back, too.

Figure 2

Figure 3

The Actress

It tries to be businesslike, but this bag's dreamy silk lining and sophisticated design give it away. It's totally Grace Kelly, movie star.

Special Tools
or Materials

Cord, 1 yard

Specialty yarn, 1 ball

Chenille (embroidery) needle

Button

Fabric

Decorator fabric; vintage silk lining

HANDMADE BY
Valerie Shrader

How It's Different

It's not! Follow the pattern instructions for construction.

How It's Special

Add the couching before you apply the interfacing or buckram to the front. (Buckram was used instead of interfacing on this bag for additional structure.) Couching is simple—all you do is stitch the cording in place using the decorative yarn. (See page 26 for an illustration.) Use a chenille needle with a large eye so you can thread the variegated yarn through it.

The Ballerina

Hip Index
Totally Elegant

Bag Pattern
The Flirt

Doesn't she look enchanting in her tutu? Bravissimo!

Special Tools or Materials

Hair canvas, ½ yard

Tulle, 1¼ yards

2 snaps

Fabric

Rayon/polyester blend; synthetic taffeta lining

HANDMADE BY
Nathalie Mornu

How It's Different

Use hair canvas instead of buckram to interface this handbag. Assemble the handbag as in The Flirt instructions and stitch each side of the top to the 4-inch mark. Turn under the raw edges ½ inch and press. Make the lining in the same fashionable way.

How It's Special

Cut two lengths of tulle that are each 1¼ x 45 inches. Gather each length of tulle until it fits the opening in the handbag. With the handbag wrong side out, pin the tulle in place, placing the edge of the tulle on the seamline. Stitch the tulle in place ¼ inch from the edge.

Turn the purse right side out. Place the lining inside the bag, wrong sides together. Pin and stitch the lining to the bag along both sides of the opening, matching the other line of stitching as closely as possible. Sew on the snaps.

The Sweetheart of the Rodeo

Every girl needs a few ruffles in her life, especially if she hangs around with cowboys.

Special Tools or Materials

1-inch bias tape maker

Button

Fabric

Decorator denim; cotton accents and lining

How It's Different

It's not! Follow the pattern instructions for construction.

HANDMADE BY
Valerie Shrader

How It's Special

Add the two layers of ruffles by cutting strips that are at least twice as long as the length of the bag. In this bag, the bottom layer of cotton (which is also the lining material) is ½ inch wider than the top layer of denim. Face each ruffle before gathering. Then, use the bias tape maker (run, don't walk to get one, because they're a mighty fine tool) to make the strips to cover the edges of the top ruffle; the raw edges of the cotton ruffle are covered by the denim ruffle. Apply the ruffled beautification before you construct the bag, after you've applied the interfacing to the bag piece.

Pattern

Materials & Tools

Fabric, ½ yard

Lining, ½ yard

Buckram, ¼ yard

Fusible interfacing, ½ yard

Sewing kit

Pieces to Cut

Bag—2 of fabric, 2 of lining, 2 of interfacing

Bottom—1 of fabric, 1 of lining, 1 of buckram, 1 of interfacing

Straps—2 of fabric, each 3 x 17 inches; 2 of interfacing, each 3 x 17 inches

Remember to use ½-inch seam allowances.

Handbag Basics on pages 16–23.

The Vessel

Put everything in here. The vessel can take it, and then you can take it all with you—in style.

How You Make It

1. Trim the seam allowances from the buckram and place it between the seamlines on the fabric bottom piece. Apply the interfacing to the fabric bottom piece, sandwiching the buckram between the fabric and the interfacing. Apply the interfacing to the wrong side of the fabric bag pieces.

2. With right sides together, pin the two fabric bag pieces together along the sides. Stitch the seams and press them open.

3. Find the center of the fabric bottom piece by folding it lengthwise; mark the centerline at both side edges. Pin the fabric bottom piece to the bag, right sides together, matching the marks on the bottom piece to the side seams of the bag. Stitch to within ½ inch of the first corner, pivot the fabric, and continue to stitch around the bottom in this manner, pivoting at each corner (figure 2). Reinforce the corners with another row of stitching if you're feeling insecure. Trim the corners. Press the seams toward the bag and turn the bag right side out.

4. Make **Strap A** from **Handbag Basics**. First apply the interfacing to the wrong sides of each strap piece. Fold one strap piece in half lengthwise, right sides together. Stitch the length of the strap, pivot at the corner, and stitch across one end. Repeat for the second strap. Turn the straps inside out through the open end. Trim the seams from the short ends so each strap has two open ends with raw edges. Press both pieces flat with seam in the center.

5. Pin the straps to the bag, right sides together, each end of the strap about 3½ inches from the side seams. (You'll be looking at the seam in the straps if you've got it right.) Look at the illustrations for **Strap A** in **Handbag Basics** if you need a reminder.

Figure 1

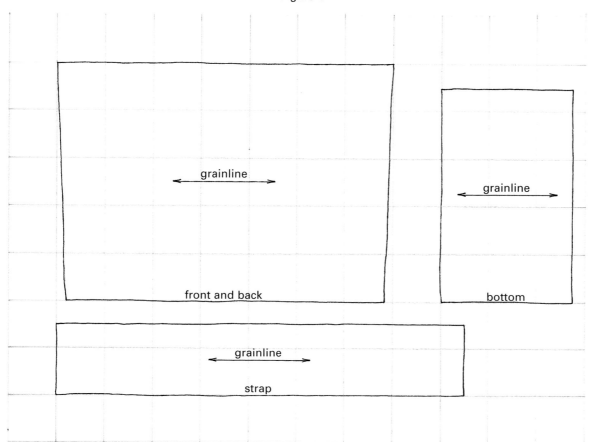

grainline

front and back

grainline

bottom

grainline

strap

1 square = 2 inches

6. Now prepare the lining like **Lining A** in **Handbag Basics**. Stitch the lining bag pieces together and then stitch the lining bottom piece to the bag lining, as in steps 2 and 3 above, but *leave a 5-inch section open in the bottom*. Trim the seams and press them open. Leave the lining wrong side out.

7. With right sides together, place the lining over the bag and align the top edges. Pin the bag to the lining, making sure the handles are lying flat between the fabric and the lining and not somehow caught in the seam allowance. Match the side seams. Stitch, then clip the curves.

8. Turn the bag right side out through the 5-inch opening in the bottom of the lining. Stitch the opening closed by hand or machine. Push the lining into the bag and press the top edge. Topstitch if you feel like it.

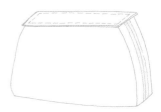

Figure 2

Hot Tip

If you're using heavy fabric and/or interfacing, it may be easiest to pin and stitch one side of the bottom at a time in step 3. Then pin and stitch the next side instead of pivoting at the corners as you sew.

The Déjà Vu

Hip Index
Somewhere in Between

Bag Pattern
The Vessel

Seems like I've been here before. . . past meets present in this handbag, with its modern accents and retro fabric.

Special Tools or Materials

Zipper, 12 inches

Grommets, 2 that are ¼ inch and 2 that are ⁷⁄₁₆ inch
Grommet setting tools

Fabric

Vintage barkcloth; upholstery accents; cotton lining

HANDMADE BY
Valerie Shrader

How It's Different

This bag's got a little of everything so it will do a lot of whatever. The pattern has been enlarged to take full advantage of the repeats in the fabric. Add grommets to the bottom border; this one was cut using the bottom 3 inches of the bag pattern. Stitch the border to the bag as if it were an appliqué, so the barkcloth is visible through the grommets. Make the straps like **Strap A** in the **Handbag Basics** (page 19), but add the grommets, stitch the straps flat on the purse, and then fold them in half at about the 3-inch mark. Then stitch the handles to form a narrower strap.

The lining has a couple of surprises—two pockets, one a patch pocket that's stitched into sections to hold those pesky pens that try to hide in the bottom of your pocketbook. The other is a slash pocket, complete with zipper; learn how to make both of these **pockets** in **Handbag Basics** (pages 20–21). Add the pockets to the lining before it's constructed and slipped into the bag, wrong sides together, and basted along the top edge of the bag. The facing will cover the raw edges so none are visible inside the purse.

Facing? What facing? The Déjà Vu has a zipper installed into a facing that is cut using the top 3 inches of the bag pattern. Add the **zipper** to the facing as described in the **Handbag Basics** (page 18), with the length of stitching in step 1 altered to accommodate your zipper and your facing. Fold the ends of the facing right sides together and stitch across the ends (figure 1). Adding the facing is the last step in the construction. Open the zipper and turn the facing inside out and upside down so the zipper is at the bottom. Slip the facing over the bag, right sides together, and pin (figure 2). Stitch. Turn the facing to the inside of the bag, and topstitch if you want to.

Figure 1

Figure 2

How It's Special

The grommets here are totally decorative. Add if the spirit moves you.

The Bubble Bag

*Little bubbles, big bubbles, blue bubbles, yellow bubbles.
Grab onto your bag before it floats away!*

Special Tools
or Materials

Button

Fabric

Decorator jacquard;
  lame´ lining

How It's Different

The Bubble Bag has lots of the little extras that really make your day. It's got a great front **pocket** for the cell phone and an awfully cute **flap** and button closure. You can figure out how to add both of these things in **Handbag Basics** (pages 16–23); they need to be in place before you line the bag.

How It's Special

No, two different pieces of fabric weren't used in this project. It's just one piece of great material, which just happens to have reversed colors on the "wrong" side. It makes for a lot of fun, doesn't it?

The funky strap with hexagonal medallions really makes it, though. To get 13 finished hexagons, simply cut 26 pieces. These are sort of 2½ by 2½ inches. Put two of the pieces together, folding in the raw edges, and stitch together to make each hexagon. Then, make the strap by stitching the finished hexagons to one another in a completely casual nonchalant kind of way. Add the strap as instructed for The Vessel.

HANDMADE BY
Kelledy Francis

The Blooming Bag

This bag is bursting with petals. But please don't pick the flowers.

Special Tools or Materials

None!

Fabric

Faux suede; satin lining

How It's Different

There's no fusible interfacing in this bag, just the buckram in the bottom. The lining is composed of two pieces; overlap and sew them together so there's no bulky seam. Line the upper part of the bag with faux suede and the bottom portion with satin. The suede portion extends about 5 inches down into the bag.

Oh yeah—one more thing. Use **Strap B** from **Handbag Basics** (page 19) rather than **Strap A**.

HANDMADE BY
Joan K. Morris

How It's Special

Cut 36 petals (use the template in figure 1) that are about 2¼ x 2¼ inches. Make a 1¼-inch cut down the center of each petal, beginning at the flat edge. Overlap the edges you just cut and tack them together to create the gentle curve of the petals. Before you begin to construct the bag, add the petals to the front, starting at the bottom. Stitch six petals across the bottom, evenly spaced. Repeat to make six rows; be sure the raw edges of the petals on the top row are even with the raw edges of the bag. When you're stitching the side seams, be careful not to catch the petals in the seams.

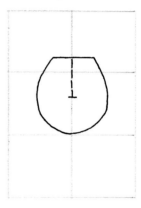

Figure 1

1 square = 2 inches

The Starry Starry Night

Beaded stars scattered across a velvet sky lit by a golden shaft of moonlight. The essence of romance, this bag. But hip too.

Special Tools or Materials

Beaded trim, ¼ yard

Seed beads

Beading needle

Beading floss

Metallic cord, ⅜ yard

Fabric

Velvet; synthetic crepe-backed
  satin lining

How It's Different

This gem of a bag is a scaled-down version of The Vessel;
its finished size is about 6 x 5 inches.

How It's Special

Decorate the front of the bag with trim and beads before you
construct the bag. Use invisible thread to add the beaded trim
first, then stitch on groups of seed beads. Add the cord as you
would the strap for The Vessel.

HANDMADE BY
Valerie Shrader
&
Terry Taylor

The Traveler

This bag zips up and goes the distance with you—uptown, downtown, or across the globe.

Materials & Tools

Fabric, ½ yard

Lining, ½ yard

Buckram, ¼ yard

Fusible interfacing, ½ yard

Zipper, 9 inches

¼-inch cording, 1 yard

Masking tape

Chopstick

Sewing kit

Pieces to Cut

Bag—2 of fabric, 2 of lining, 2 of interfacing

Zipper Placket—1 of fabric, 1 of lining, 1 of interfacing

Gusset—1 of fabric, 1 of lining, 1 of buckram

Handles—2 of fabric, each ½ x 18 inches

Remember to use ½-inch seam allowances.

Handbag Basics on pages 16–23.

How You Make It

1. Apply the interfacing to the wrong side of the fabric bag pieces, as well as to the zipper placket.

2. To put in the **zipper**, cut the zipper placket in half lengthwise. Then use the same technique as demonstrated in **Handbag Basics**. Stitch 1 inch from each side, leaving the middle open. Press the seam open, turning the raw edges under. Place the zipper under the pressed edges and pin in place. With your zipper foot, begin stitching at the top of the zipper and continue down one side until you reach the bottom. Lift the zipper foot, leaving the needle in the down position, and pivot the fabric. Lower the zipper foot and stitch across the bottom. Pivot again, stitch back up the other side of the zipper, pivot, and stitch across the top. Make sure the zipper runs freely.

3. Make **Strap C** as in **Handbag Basics**. Fold each handle piece together lengthwise, right sides together. Adjust the width of the

seam so the cord can *just* slide into the strip after the seam is sewn. Stitch across one short end, pivot, and stitch down the long side. Turn the handle right side out. Now that you've turned the strap, trim the seam from the short end so you have two open ends. Cut the cord into two 16-inch pieces. To get the cord into the handle, use the not-very-technical-yet-highly-efficient method discussed in **Handbag Basics**: Tape one end of the cord to the end of the chopstick, and scoot the chopstick through the handle. Once the cord is through, remove the chopstick.

4. Center the cord inside each handle piece; there should be excess fabric on each end. Press this fabric flat and fold the end under about ¼ inch.

5. Decide where you want to place the straps on the body of the bag— remember the ½-inch seam allowance on the bag. Pin and stitch the straps in place.

6. To install the zipper placket, mark the top center of one of the bag pieces. Then find and mark the center of the long side of the zipper placket. With right sides together, line up the center marks and pin the zipper placket to the bag. You'll need to ease the two pieces together; you might find it's easier to pin the first section of the seam and then ease around the curves as you sew. Begin and end the seam ½ inch away from the edge; be careful not to stitch the handles into the seam. Repeat to stitch the placket to the other bag piece (figure 2). Clip the curves.

7. To install the gusset, baste the buckram to the wrong side of the gusset, stitching at the seamline. Trim the buckram close to the seamline. Open the zipper about 1 inch. Place the end of the gusset on one end of the zipper placket, right sides together. Stitch across, beginning and ending at the ½-inch seamline. Repeat to stitch the other end of the gusset to the zipper placket.

8. Now, turn the work so you stitch around one side to the bottom of the bag, continuing around the seamline begun when you added the zipper placket. Pivot at the corners and stitch until you reach the other end of the zipper placket. (Clipping a scant ¼ inch into the seam of the

Figure 1

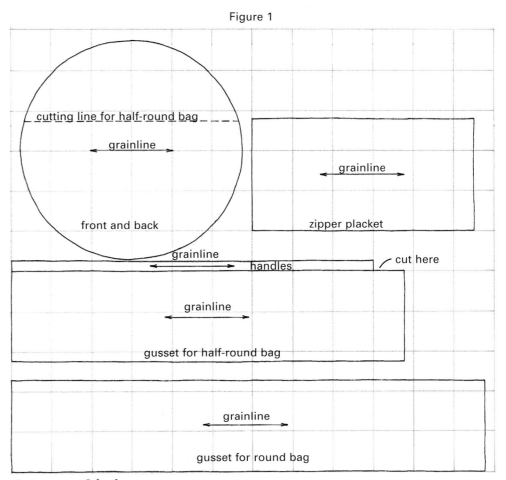

cutting line for half-round bag

grainline

front and back

grainline

zipper placket

grainline

handles

cut here

grainline

gusset for half-round bag

grainline

gusset for round bag

1 square = 2 inches

gusset may help you ease around the curves.) Repeat to stitch the other side (figure 3). Trim the corners. Fully open the zipper and turn the bag right side out. Press the seams as best you can.

9. Now make the lining. (This is basically **Lining B** in **Handbag Basics**.) Begin by making the zipper placket lining as in step 2, but don't install the zipper, of course. Construct the rest of the lining as in steps 6 and 7. Press the lining seams open.

10. With the lining wrong side out, place it inside the bag. Whipstitch the lining to the zipper tape. Try to hide your stitches as best you can.

Figure 2

Figure 3

Cool Alternative

Make the round bag by following these instructions, too. Lotsa room for lotsa stuff in that one!

The Op Art Carpetbag

This handbag gets its special glow from a fantastic fabric choice, textured faille with an artsy design.

Special Tools and Materials

None!

Fabric

Decorator faille; decorator cotton accents; satin lining

How It's Different

It's not, really; this handbag was just constructed from two different fabrics, the faille for the body of the bag and the cotton for the gusset, placket, and straps.

HANDMADE BY
Joan K. Morris

The Funky Chicken

No, your purse does not have to be soft and cuddly. This one is edgy...but in a friendly sort of way.

Special Tools or Materials

1-inch chicken wire

Craft wire

Wire cutters

Needle-nose pliers

Fabric

Chicken wire; nylon lining

How It's Different

Well obviously, this one *is* different. Use the pattern pieces for The Traveler to cut out the lining fabric. Pull a little switcheroo and use the zipper placket for the base of the bag and the gusset for the top and sides of the bag. (Interesting how that works out, isn't it?) Stitch the sides, bottom, and back of the lining, right sides together, and machine hem the curved edge. Hem the curved edge of the front panel before sewing it to the lining along the straight bottom edge, right sides together.

Place the chicken wire on top of the bag pattern piece and clip the wire along the seamline. Cut two pieces of chicken wire this way, one for the front and one for the back. Tape the gusset and zipper placket pattern pieces together into a long side panel and clip this shape from the chicken wire. Use the craft wire to form three frames, using the perimeter of the bag pattern as a guide.

HANDMADE BY
Stacey Budge

Fold the clipped edges of the back around one of the frames (figure 1), and fold the clipped edges of the front around another one. Attach the side panel to the frame around the back piece and fold the wires closed. Fold the clipped edges of the remaining side panel around the third frame. Attach this frame to the front at the bottom edges by forming simple hinges with loops of craft wire.

Cut a 26-inch length of craft wire and fold it into a 13-inch length so there are loops at both ends; the clipped edges should be in the middle. Starting 1 inch from the end of a loop, use the craft wire to wrap tightly around the length of folded wire, leaving a 1-inch loop at the other end. (In the process you'll enclose the raw ends that are folded to the middle.) Bend the wrapped wire into the shape of a handle.

Cut two 16-inch pieces of wire and fold each in half. Attach to the handbag at the top where you want to attach the handle, with the folded side facing the front. Twist it over the front of the frame and bend the folded end down to create a latch. Wrap the raw ends of the latch pieces around the back frame. Repeat to attach the other latch piece (figure 2). Attach the handle to the latch pieces using a small piece of wire. Tack the lining to the inside of the wire frame with needle and thread.

Figure 1

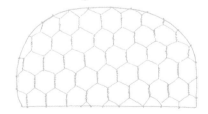

Figure 2

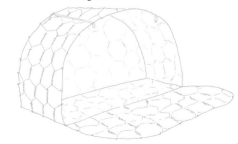

The Hipster

Well, here it is. The finale. Three coordinating fabrics so hot that they're positively cool.

Special Tools or Materials

Embroidery floss

Embroidery needle

Fabric

Decorator cotton (bag and lining)

HANDMADE BY
Valerie Shrader

How It's Different

Well, there's not much, really. This is, of course, the round version of The Traveler, and it's got a little zipper pull added before the gusset is sewn to the placket. Make a zipper pull like a strap, really—say **Strap A** in **Handbag Basics** (page 19). This one's just about 1 x 1 inch finished.

Make the straps like **Strap A** too, come to think of it, but stitch them flat onto the purse and then fold them in half at about the 2-inch mark. Stitch to form a narrower strap.

How It's Special

Have some fun with embroidery stitches to accent the designs on your fabric. In this project, simple running stitches and French knots add fanciful little flourishes. (See page 26 for illustratiions.)

Hot Tip

This bag is made from three coordinating fabrics: one for each of the sides and a sassy stripe for the gusset and zipper placket.

Gallery of Totally Hip Handbags

Moo Roo
Moo Moo Fou Fou, 2004
8 x 2 x 5 ½ in. (20.3 x 5 x 14 cm)
Satin; ostrich feathers, caviar
bead trim
PHOTO BY JOE MEDIA

Irina Nikolaivna
Moscow Mink, 2004
7⁷⁄₁₆ x 8 x 2 in. (18.9 x 20.3 x 5 cm)
Faux suede; hand quilted; beads,
mink, and mother-of-pearl
PHOTO BY DAVID FAIRCHILD

Denton F. Kump/for Poesis
Twisted Tria, 2004
10 x 16 x 3 in. (25.4 x 40.6 x 7.6 cm)
Printed cotton
PHOTO BY STEVE HELBER

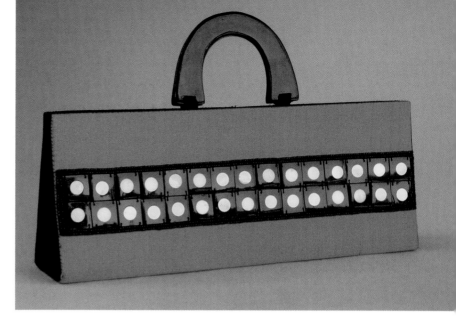

Christine Brown
Dominoes, 2004
5 x 12 x 2½ in. (12.7 x 30.5 x 6.4 cm)
Silk; cut horn inlaid with mother-of-pearl dots
PHOTO BY ARTIST

Jennifer Nakatsu Arntson
Space-Blue Ripple Appliqué Airline Shoulder Tote, 2004
10 x 13¼ x 5½ in. (25.4 x 33.7 x 14 cm)
Upholstery-grade vinyl; hand-cut and stitched appliqué; laminated, edgestitched, and riveted shoulder strap
PHOTO BY ARTIST

JD Brown
Pretty Tied Up, 2004
8½ x 11½ x 4 in. (21.6 x 29.2 x 10.2 cm)
Microfiber; metal buckles and clasp
PHOTO BY ARTIST

Christina Case
Woman Seeking Man, 2003
5 x 7 x ½ in. (12.7 x 17.8 x 6.4 cm)
Stoneware, newsprint, acrylic; lace, beads, and oil pencil
PHOTO BY SUZANNE KAUFMAN

Gena Ollendieck
Make the Shift...Give,
2004
9 x 8 x 4¼ in.
(22.9 x 20.3 x 10.8 cm)
Tan leather; inlaid and
altered found objects;
functional doors
PHOTO BY LARRY SANDERS

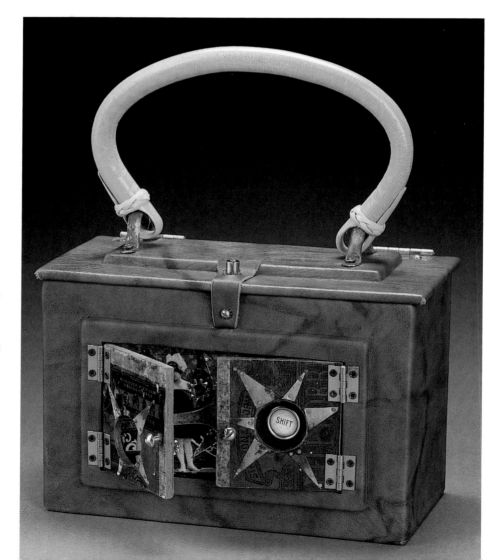

Kim Kulow-Jones and
Douglas W. Jones /Random Orbit
Handbag Grouping, 2003
Dimensions vary
Recycled tin cans, turned wood tops and feet,
leather, tassels, ball chain; paint and gold leaf
PHOTO BY JERRY ANTHONY

Lori M. Sandstedt
Mixt Metaphor: Hot!, 2003
7 x 8 x 3 in. (17.8 x 20.3 x 7.6 cm)
Cigar box; collage from vintage
ephemera; handle from porcelain
faucet fixture
PHOTO BY STEVE MELTZER

Carol Gaczek
Love Shack "Stone Bag," 2004
11½ x 6 x 5 in. (29.2 x 15.2 x 12.7 cm)
Ceramic sculpture (birdhouse); single
fired, hand carved, and stamped
PHOTO BY ARTIST

Shula Paz
Funky Denim Handbag, 2004
11 x 9½ x 2 in. (27.9 x 24.1 x 5 cm)
Hand-built ceramic; low-fire glazes; feather trim
PHOTO BY KARI PEJOVICH

Wendy Stevens
Penne Purse, 2003
5 x 9 x 3½ in. (12.7 x 22.9 x 8.9 cm)
Embossed and highlighted stainless
steel, leather gussets and strap; hinged
with pivot closure; hand fabricated
PHOTO BY PAUL HAZI

Wendy Stevens
Buona Sera Handbag, 2002
4 x 3½ x 1¾ in. (10.2 x 8.9 x 4.4 cm)
Perforated stainless steel, leather gussets,
double handles, flap closure; hand fabricated
PHOTO BY PAUL HAZI

Erica Shaver
Seduction, 1999
8 x 4 x ¼ in. (20.3 x 10.2 x .6 cm)
Sterling silver, steel; cast and
fabricated; freshwater pearls
PHOTO BY ARTIST

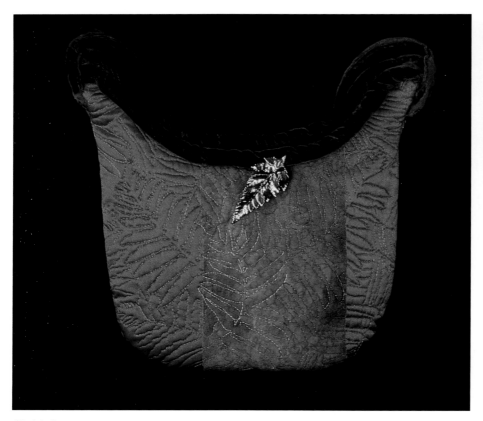

Skybird
Fond of Ferns, 2003
11 x 12 x 2 in. (27.9 x 30.5 x 5 cm)
Silk, rayon, velvet; machine quilted; copper-plated fern frond
PHOTO BY ARTIST

Linda and Opie O'Brien/Burnt Offerings
From Harvest to Handbag:
The Gourd Purse, 2003
9 x 7 x 5 in. (22.9 x 17.8 x 12.7 cm)
Lagenaria gourd; pyrography; vintage
dominoes, coins, beads, and joss paper
PHOTO BY STUDIO ROSSI

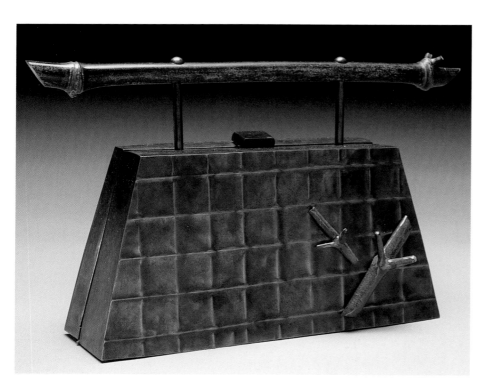

Lori Müller
Bamboo Handbag, 2004
6 x 8 x 2½ in. (15.2 x 20.3 x 6.4 cm)
Copper and bamboo; liver of sulfur
patina; cast and enameled
PHOTO BY LAUCH MCKENZIE

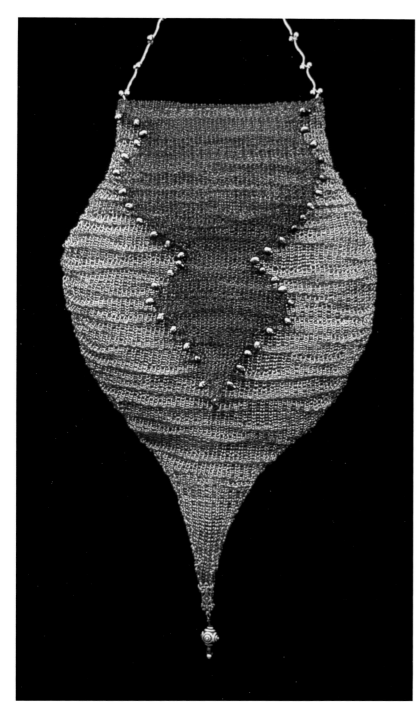

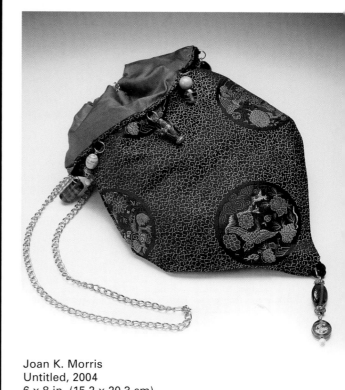

Joan K. Morris
Untitled, 2004
6 x 8 in. (15.2 x 20.3 cm)
Silk brocade; bead accents
PHOTO BY KEITH WRIGHT

Sharmen Liao
Amphora, 2001
11 x 6½ x 1 in. (27.9 x 16.5 x 2.5 cm)
Loom-knitted wire mesh and silk lining; pearls
PHOTO BY ARTIST

Moo Roo
Catherine, 2004
7½ x 3 x 5 in. (19 x 7.6 x 12.7 cm)
Turquoise and cheetah print silk charmeuse; custom crystal spray jewel
PHOTO BY JOE MEDIA

Irina Nikolaivna
Trip to Japan, 2003
11¼ x 5 in. (28.6 x 12.7 cm)
Silk fabric and thread; hand embroidered; seed beads

PHOTOS BY DAVID FAIRCHILD

Kathy Ticho
Square Dance, 2003
6 x 9 x 5½ in. (15.2 x 22.9 x 14 cm)
Wool; hand knit and felted; button closure
PHOTO BY ERIC HERZOG

Elizabeth A. Schock
Dickie's Delight, 2003
16 x 10 x 5 in. (40.6 x 25.4 x 12.7 cm)
Crocheted stainless steel wire, copper,
and pen shells; enameled
PHOTO BY ARTIST

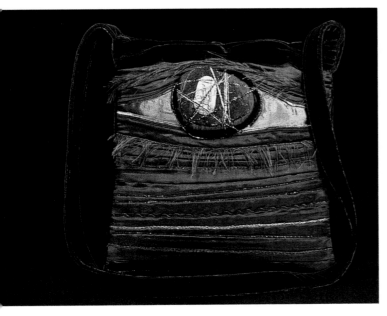

Skybird
Eye of Isis, 2003
10 x 9 x 1 in. (25.4 x 22.9 x 2.5 cm)
Silk, velvet, couched yarns; hand-wrapped, beaded
embellishment of silk with stamped polymer clay
PHOTO BY ARTIST

Barbara Zaretsky
Untitled, n.d.
6½ x 7½ in. (16.5 x 17.8 cm)
Found black velvet bag with gold metal clasp;
beaded and embroidered; plastic beads, cotton floss,
and velvet cording
PHOTO BY KEITH WRIGHT

Lisa Klakulak
Group Shot of Spring 2004 Series, 2004
Various dimensions
Wool; hand felted, naturally dyed; appliquéd,
machine and hand stitched
PHOTO BY JOHN LUCUS, TTV PHOTOSERVICES

Linda MacMichael and Tim Clark
Ciao, 2003
8½ x 7½ x ½ in. (21.6 x 19 x 1.3 cm)
Silk and faux suede; topstitched and pieced;
handmade Kumihimo braid
PHOTO BY TOM MILLS

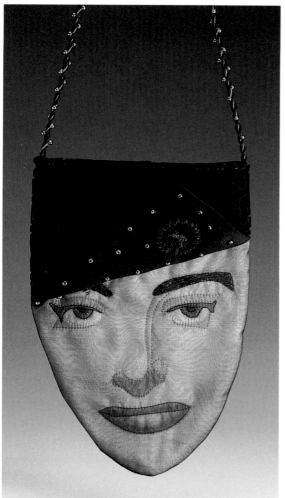

Kathleen Dustin
Evening Purse, 2003
4 x 6 x 2 in. (10.2 x 15.2 x 5 cm)
Polymer clay, adjustable shoulder cord;
sculpted, baked, hand rendered; layered,
sanded, and polished
PHOTO BY GEORGE POST

Linda MacMichael and Tim Clark
Mommy, 2004
10 x 7 x ¾ in. (25.4 x 17.8 x 1.9 cm)
Silk and faux suede; inkjet photo
transfer, hand and machine
embroidery; handmade
Kumihimo strap, beading
PHOTO BY TOM MILLS

Allison P. Sanders
Faces, 2004
13 x 6 x 2 in. (33 x 15.2 x 5 cm)
Stained glass; copper wire, vintage earring clasp
PHOTO BY ARICCA VOLK

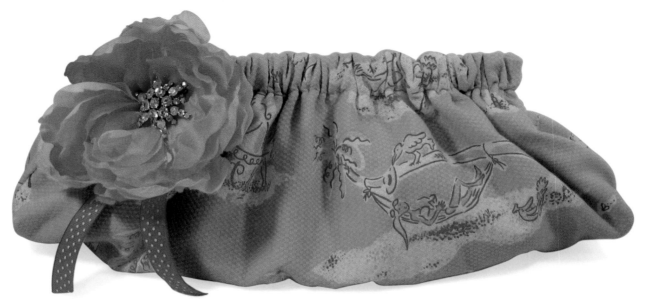

Emily Hsu and Margaret Gates Morrow/Myna Bags
Carrie Clutch, 2004
6 x 10 x 3 in. (15.2 x 25.4 x 7.6 cm)
Cotton pique novelty print; flower with rhinestone pin, grosgrain ribbon
PHOTO BY EMILY HSU

Torie Nguyen/Totinette
La Parisienne, 2004
7 x 12 in. (17.8 x 30.5 cm)
Cotton and denim; button closure
PHOTO BY CHRISTINE GEORGE

Adrien Lucas
Liquid Paisley, 1999
12 x 12 x 3 in. (30.5 x 30.5 x 7.6 cm)
Taffeta; embroidery; satin rosettes and vintage
Czechoslovakian beads
PHOTO BY BRUCK ECKER

Metric Conversion Chart

Inches	Millimeters (mm)/ Centimeters (cm)
⅛	3 mm
3/16	5 mm
¼	6 mm
5/16	8 mm
⅜	9.5 mm
7/16	1.1 cm
½	1.3 cm
9/16	1.4 cm
⅝	1.6 cm
11/16	1.7 cm
¾	1.9 cm
13/16	2.1 cm
⅞	2.2 cm
15/16	2.4 cm
1	2.5 cm
1½	3.8 cm
2	5 cm
2½	6.4 cm
3	7.6 cm
3½	8.9 cm
4	10.2 cm
4½	11.4 cm
5	12.7 cm
5½	14 cm
6	15.2 cm
6½	16.5 cm
7	17.8 cm
7½	19 cm
8	20.3 cm

Inches	Millimeters (mm)/ Centimeters (cm)
8½	21.6 cm
9 (¼ yard)	22.9 cm
9½	24.1 cm
10	25.4 cm
10½	26.7 cm
11	27.9 cm
11½	29.2 cm
12	30.5 cm
12½	31.8 cm
13	33 cm
13½	34.3 cm
14	35.6 cm
14½	36.8 cm
15	38.1 cm
15½	39.4 cm
16	40.6 cm
16½	41.9 cm
17	43.2 cm
17½	44.5 cm
18 (½ yard)	45.7 cm
18½	47 cm
19	48.3 cm
19½	49.5 cm
20	50.8 cm
20½	52 cm
21	53.3
21½	54.6
22	55 cm
22½	57.2 cm

Inches	Millimeters (mm)/ Centimeters (cm)
23	58.4 cm
2 ½	59.7 cm
24	61 cm
24½	62.2 cm
25	63.5 cm
25½	64.8 cm
26	66 cm
26½	67.3 cm
27	68.6 cm
27½	69.9 cm
28	71.1 cm
28½	72.4 cm
29	73.7 cm
29½	74.9 cm
30	76.2 cm
30½	77.5 cm
31	78.7 cm
31½	80 cm
32	81.3 cm
32½	82.6 cm
33	83.8 cm
33½	85 cm
34	86.4 cm
34½	87.6 cm
35	88.9 cm
35½	90.2 cm
36 (1 yard)	91.4 cm

Acknowledgments

I'm here to tell you that a girl (and heck, the occasional guy too) sure loves a handbag. The talented designers you'll read about on these pages really had fun with the projects and their enthusiasm for the book was infectious. Thanks so much to all of you; words can't express my gratitude for the time and the care and the creativity you gave to these fabulous bags. You go girls!

My technical consultant deserves a special mention because she was just so awesome. From making paper models to sewing muslin prototypes, she hung in there with a smile and remarkable good cheer, considering she did it all in about two days. Thanks, Joanie, for all of your help.

Finally, a shout out to the folks at Lark Books for believing in the project; my great photographer, Keith Wright, who's a whiz behind the camera and knows all the cool Internet radio stations; and my unbelievably talented art director, Susan McBride, who can do just about anything very very well. I'm extremely grateful to all for this really hip—and totally beautiful—book.

Technical Consultant

The artistic endeavors of technical consultant and project designer **Joan K. Morris** have led her down many successful creative paths, including ceramics and costume design for motion pictures. She is currently the owner of a coffee house in Asheville, North Carolina. Joan has contributed projects for numerous Lark books, including *Beautiful Ribbon Crafts* (2003), *Gifts For Baby* (2003), *Halloween* (2003), *Creating Fantastic Vases* (2003), *Hardware Style* (2003), *The Michaels Book of Arts & Crafts* (2003), and many more.

Project Designers

Stacey Budge is an art director at Lark Books. When she's not designing books, she can be found crafting and gardening at her home in Asheville, North Carolina.

Kelledy Francis is originally from Orlando, Florida, where she realized that designing and sewing is in her blood. At 16 years old, she went to study with her grandmother, Fawn Zeller, who was a world-renowned historical costumer. The experience intensified her interest in fabric and fashion, and she went on to receive a B.F.A. with honors from the Maryland Institute, College of Art, in fiber arts. Kelledy recently moved to Asheville, North Carolina from Chicago, Illinois, in search of better weather and less traffic. She is currently pursuing a masters of fine arts at Western Carolina University in Cullowhee, North Carolina.

Megan Kirby is an art director and project designer living in Asheville, North Carolina. She designs her own clothes.

Diana Light is a D. Light-ful (get it?) artist who has an uncanny ability to make everything she touches look absolutely fabulous and instantly cool. She specializes in functional art, turning any object into something beautiful and useful. Diana has designed many projects for many (many) Lark books. Contact her at dianalight@hotmail.com.

Susan McBride is an artist, designer and art director for Lark Books. She has created many projects for Lark books, including *Altered Art* (2004), *Artful Eggs* (2004), *Halloween* (2003), and many others. To see more of her work, go to susanmcbridedesign.com.

Nathalie Mornu's first sewing attempt in a seventh-grade home economics class was a floral purse with round, clear plastic handles. She hated it, and let it languish unfinished in a closet for years! Nathalie has also made projects for other Lark books, including *Decorating Your First Apartment* (2002), *Creative Scarecrows* (2004), and *The Weekend Crafter: Making Gingerbread Houses* (2004).

Allison Chandler Smith calls the beautiful mountains of Western North Carolina home. She is a self-taught crafter and designer whose work has been featured in numerous Lark books, including *Summer Style* (2003), *Decorating Your First Apartment* (2002), and *The Michaels Book of Arts & Crafts* (2003). She recently authored Lark's *Girls World Book of Bath and Beauty* (2004). Samples of her work can be seen on her website at www.lemondropdesign.com.

Terry Taylor is a versatile project coordinator and editor at Lark Books. He is a prolific designer and exhibiting artist, working in media from metals and jewelry to paper crafts and mosaics. Terry has written several books for Lark, including *Altered Art* (2004), *Artful Eggs* (2004), and *The Weekend Crafter: Paper Crafting* (2002). He is co-author of Lark's well-received children's series: *The Book of Wizard Crafts* (2001); *The Book of Wizard Parties* (2002); and *Wizard Magic* (2003). At last count, Terry's project designs have been published in over 60 Lark books.

A NOTE ABOUT SUPPLIERS

Usually, the supplies you need for making the projects in Lark books can be found at your local craft supply store, discount mart, home improvement center, or retail shop relevant to the topic of the book. Occasionally, however, you may need to buy materials or tools from specialty suppliers. In order to provide you with the most up-to-date information, we have created a list of suppliers on our website, which we update on a regular basis. Visit us at www.larkbooks.com, click on "Craft Supply Sources," and then click on the relevant topic. You will find numerous companies listed with their web address and/or mailing address and phone number.

Artist Index

Index